GOD (ELOHIM) IS A BLACK MAN

"YAHOSHUAH IS A BLACK MAN"

Dr Trevor Udennis DD
Copyright © 2017
1st Edition 2017

GOD (ELOHIM) IS A BLACK MAN

Copyright © 2017 by Dr Trevor Udennis
First published in the UK by EasyRway Ltd 2017
1st Edition

www.Hebrewapostolic.com

All scripture quotations in this publication are from the King James Authorised Version of the Holy Bible
'Please note emphasis where added to scriptures'

Printed in the USA
First Printing 2017

by Dr. Trevor H. Udennis D.D.
ISBN-13: 978-1548644666 (CreateSpace-Assigned)
ISBN-10: 1548644668

Dedication

This book is first dedicated to Elohim the giver of life and inspiration without whom this work would not exist. Secondly my thanks goes to my family: Julia my wife and my two sons (Theron and Danel). They are so supportive of my work and ministry that I can only acknowledge them with the deepest of thanks to Elohim.

This book was inspired in the tropical Island of Antigua where this issue became a live topic of interest and was preached far and wide among the people of the Island. By now most of the people on the Island knows that, "God is a black man."

It seems somewhat incredibly interesting; to find where the strong desire Caucasian people have for God (Elohim) to be a white man is coming from? When they found God centuries ago through the true Hebrews, He was black and a Jew.

Just a few short centuries later, He is blonde haired and blue eyed. How is it possible that the image of God (Elohim) who is Yahoshuah the Messiah, born in North East Africa from a Semitic (black woman) from a black tribe (Judah) could bear a blonde haired blue eyed son? Perhaps it's a joke?

No there has actually been a deliberate attempt to deceive the world into believing God (Elohim) is white, but no, God is a Black man and I can prove it.

If you have further questions, contact EasyRway Ltd. Our regular business hours are Mon-Thurs. 9:30 am – 6 pm GMT, and Friday 10:30 am – 5 pm. During these hours, you can reach us by phone, or email. Outside of these hours, either call and leave a message or email us.

Email: **hebrewapostolic@gmail.com**
Website **www.hebrewapostolic.com**

Contents

Foreword

This book was written as a follow on from the book, "Black skin royal identity" which came about due to the need of Hebrews for a revelation and understanding about their identity.

In this book, we take another significant step by unwrapping teachings that enables a Hebrew to master the Book that belongs to them, for "The Bible" is not a gentile book, but a book given by Elohim to His people. So in this book, we equip Hebrew Apostolics with the knowledge that is required to know their God (Elohim).

This book is also designed to help pastors to develop the work of Yah by understanding who their Elohim really is and how to share the understanding with those around them so that they are taught correct doctrine and are able both to stand and to rebut any incorrect teaching about the Godhead.

Our students are expected to grow from simple leaders of tens to those with greater capacity, able to lead hundreds and even thousands.

This book does however have one specific purpose; which is that we can implement what we learn to awaken Hebrew apostolics all over the world and in so doing hasten the return of our Yah and Saviour who is Yahoshuah our Messiah.

I would like to acknowledge something unusual up front, and that is that I will be using a name for our Messiah that many may think initially is wrong but is actually right. What most people do not understand is that there is no such name as Jesus in scripture, for His name is Yahoshuah.

This is the name I have chosen to use and which is different but acknowledges the original pronunciation of our Messiah's name (you can research this for yourself or read about it in another of my books specifically written to explain the reasoning about His name, but no it's not a mistake that I use this name, it's deliberate and purposeful.

Introduction

This book is not meant to read as a novel. It is a handbook that is meant for study. So as you do each lesson and make notes in the book about things you do not understand that requires further study.

This book is designed to disciple the reader, make them stronger and ensure they are more knowledgeable about the beliefs of the apostles and disciples of Yahoshuah Messiah.

Make notes about things that require you to ask questions, highlight revelations that are given to you and keep a record of what you have learned. The information is as far as possible done in a systematic way, but this work is by no means totally complete as there is only so much that can get in one book.

As you go through this book, bear in mind that the information is graded and there are audio or video lessons that can be used along-side the book to help your understanding.

Finally each chapter comes with quizzes and discussions. This allows the reader to see how well they have assimilated the information and understand how to share it most appropriately with others.

May Elohim bless you as you, "Study to show yourself approved unto Elohim, a workman that needeth not to be ashamed, rightly dividing the Word of truth" **2 Timothy 2:15**.

CHAPTER 1
A WHITE CHILD'S TESTIMONY

In 2016 on YouTube a video appeared in which a white child gave his testimony about having met God and his observation about God's colour or racial background. The video was called, **"Racist Boy Dies For 3 Minutes, Says Jesus is a N**ger."**

This pure upstanding white American boy had a vision while clinically dead which must have been for him a nightmare. The article says, *"A young white Christian boy who died on a surgeon's table during a liver transplant this past weekend, says he met Jesus Christ and He was an African American.*

Billy Landers, the son of a well-known KKK member in Mobil Alabama who was suffering from liver failure was technically dead for three minutes before being resuscitated. During that time, the thirteen year old claimed he visited the afterlife "It was all N**gers," he told WKRG news after the ordeal.

'There were a few white people, but they were just entertaining the blacks, like playing basketball. There were lots of N**ger angels watching them play basketball.' Landers said. 'Jesus was a coon too. Jesus wasn't white like Daddy says He is.'

[I asked my father 'Why is Jesus a N**ger?'] He couldn't answer. I'd been taught that God and Jesus hate N**gers. That God cursed them by turning their skin black. That they were 'mud people."

Billy's father said his son's experience has not made him question white supremacy and an Anglo-Saxon Jesus. "It's kinda disturbing to me that he came back with stories of N**ger Heaven," he told reporters, "but clearly my son is suffering from some sort of schizophrenia or something. There's no way Jesus is a N**ger. I'm going to have my boy put on anti-psychotic medications."

Interesting, yes? The boy met Jesus whom we know to be Yahoshuah. He looked black all over and when he saw Him, he said 'Jesus was a N**ger' when he met Him personally. Well that means that God's a N**ger. God's a black man, and if God is black, then let's pack up and go home, right? No wait! Billy's father may not have been noticeable affected, but Billy will be for the rest of his life. Because he now knows that God (Elohim) is a black man.

What is particularly interesting about this child's testimony is that the child has a deep investment in white supremacy but no investment in God being black and if anything, he would have liked to see God as a white man, because that is what he had been taught and told all of his life. His expectation therefore was to see a white heaven and a white God but he found the exact opposite – God's a black man.

That God is a black man cannot be birthed out of his ignorance of racism but rather his openness and apparent innocence when faced with truth are refreshing. That boy will never be the same again, no matter what drugs his doctors prescribe or what specialist he sees, he now knows that God is a black man.

Though he uses the word N**ger often in his story, it is originally from the word Niger or the region where the river Niger ran through that this word comes. This region is so called because the greatest concentrations of Hebrew people were found living in that area. The word is also akin to the Portuguese word for black, which is "Negro."

Later the word, "Niger" came to be synonymous with the Semitic black man or true Hebrew and thus the slave traders used this name as both an identifying tag and as a cuss word to be applied to the black man generally as Elohim had said in **Deuteronomy 28:37**, *"And thou shalt become an astonishment, a proverb, and a byword, among all nations whither the LORD shall lead thee."* One of the ways this has manifested is in the form of the word, "N**ger". The word, 'Nigeria' used to mean from or in the area or vicinity of the Niger (Niger-area).

The word "Negro" simply means, "black!" and is when used negatively an expression of the curse placed on the Hebrews whereby we would be referred to not by our names but through by-words or anything but our actual identities until we return to Messiah and He returns for us (**Deuteronomy 28:37**).

Biblically Simon one of Yahoshuah's disciples was also called Niger (**Acts 13:1**) as his pet name. So he was called Simon the darkie or 'Brother Midnight' and it was ok, which means there is nothing directly evil about the word, Niger (Black).

What is insidious is the attachment and disdain that has come to be associated with the word black as it is applied to a people (often referred to as N**ers) and that is what the rest of this is book is about. The racism that is behind the way that Europeans and even blacks address and deal with other blacks and even our God 'Elohim'. We will be questioning and unravelling whether this child's testimony is true (God is black?) and if so why it is both credible and feared at the same time for true Hebrews everywhere to discover the truth of who Elohim is, what He is likely to look like and be able walk in it to express His greatness and glory.

Let me add, that this child is not the only white child that Elohim has been speaking to about His colour, identity or nationality. For there are a number of YouTube videos about white children having dreams of the rapture, meeting Jesus (Yahoshuah) and finding out that He is a black man. There are also numerous confirmations that God is a black man in archeology, ancient paintings, history and the Bible that back up the claim made by Billy our example in this book.

So strap on your seatbelt as we explore the subject matter and find out who Elohim is better, what He looks like and why He chose to come in that image rather than the image of the dominant nations of the World. For if Billy is right, then everything we know is false and what we have been fed is a lie.

Quiz 1

1. How did this child come to have a vision?

2. What did he see as a scene in heaven?

3. Who were the servants and who were the served in heaven?

4. What was Billy's father's response to his vision?

5. How is the 'N' word used with reference to Elohim's people?

6. To what does the word, 'Niger' actually refer?

1. He died
2. A black Yahoshua and black angels
3. The white people were the servants and the black people the served
4. Billy needs psychotic medication
5. Negatively
6. The area of the river Niger (Niger-area)

Discussion

1. What are your observations about the attitude of some Europeans towards the use of the word, "N**ger" when talking about black people either privately or publicly?

2. What are your feelings about the use of this word and words like it when speaking of individuals and people groups?

3. Compare the attitude of Billy and his father with others you may be aware of or even know and what do you think about the attitude that produces the racist behaviour?

4. Define prejudice as opposed to racism for you personally? Then look up their meaning in a dictionary and not the difference if any.

5. What can we learn from the language, attitude and behaviour of Billy and his father?

6. What are the key things that need to change?

7. How can we practically apply these lessons to our life and live better than before we read this story?

CHAPTER 2
WHY DOES IT MATTER WHETHER ELOHIM IS BLACK OR WHITE?

The simple truth about the discussion about colour and prejudice is that it makes most people uncomfortable or else they go on to say, that the colour of people and God doesn't matter, or does it? CNN anchor Megyn Kelly hosted a discussion on the topic of Santa Claus and Jesus Christ and came out looking like a racist. On the programme "The Kelly files," She literally said, *"For all you kids watching at home, Santa is just white and Jesus too!"*

Because of this comment, later on in a different rebuttal discussion, the author Tim Wise said, *"Here's the reality. The image of a white Jesus has been used to justify enslavement, conquest, colonialism, and the genocide of indigenous peoples. There are literally millions of human beings whose lives have been snuffed out by people who conquered under the banner of a white god."*

On the same CNN discussion. He added that *"Black folks can think Jesus is black and view Christ as black, but at the end of the day, the image that has been used to dominate Christianity in this world and on this planet is the white image."* Wise was on CNN to discuss Fox's anchor Megyn Kelly's controversial claim that Santa Claus and Jesus were white when he made this comment.

Wise goes on to say, "*I think the real issue was that she made a statement of fact, not her own opinion, but fact. There's a difference between believing in Santa or Jesus or the Buddha. Buddha did not come from Kansas. Jesus was not born in a manger in central Pennsylvania. He was a man of colour* (see they already know). *And the fact that we have represented him for centuries literally as a white man speaks to the entire history of* **white supremacy***.*

We can act like it didn't happen (the scenario he just outlined that is). *We can make it the punch line of a joke. But the reality is that, this iconography* (image)*, Jesus more so than Santa, I agree with Mel here – Jesus more so than Santa is a real problem. There's a reason we've represented these icons as white. It's not a coincidence that we've done that.*"

So let me see if I got this, the reason why God is white in the first place is that He (God) is white because the Europeans learned something about our book (The Bible). They learned that religion can and was used as a method of control over Hebrew blacks during slavery. They learned that religion is effective to control slaves and if you're going to use it you must have God in your image.

A book consulted by many planters (slavers) during slavery was the Cotton Plantation Record and Account Book, which gave these instructions to overseers: "*You will find that an hour devoted every Sabbath morning to their* (the slave's) *moral and religious instruction would prove a great aid to you in bringing about a better state of things amongst the Negroes.*" That is to say, they will be easier to control.

This fact was verified through the words and actions of the Plantocracy in the Caribbean near the end of slavery when they were told by a priest as emancipation was approaching and they were nervous that everything would continue as it always had.

The priest told them that they should not worry because the Bible could be their tool to control the ex-slaves for at least the next hundred years or more. Through the simple misrepresentation of scripture it allowed the continuation of a system of oppression that depended upon Bible manipulation for its power and because a lie was in place that needed maintenance to continue to tell its story and make others believe it to be true. God had to be white to reinforce the power of the religious lie.

If God remained black as before it wouldn't work, because the slaves would not believe that a God that looked like them would treat them badly. That is why it mattered enough to change His colour to white European? Further evidence is found in the following article, *"Whites and the fear caused by white supremacy."*

They article says, *"Black people are "profoundly resilient," DeGruy posits, but the fact is, they have been traumatized... and white people are afraid. The biggest trauma whites suffer from black people... is a fear of black people, she says.*

Why the fear? Perhaps it is because white people feel afraid black people will heap upon them what they have heaped upon black people. Perhaps it is because they worry they will lose control; white supremacy is, after all, a giant system of social control. Slavery was about control, as is mass incarceration. This government was founded on the need for white people to be in control. To think about losing it (control) is way too scary.

What would happen if this nation would admit that white supremacy exists and that it has traumatized an entire race of people? What would happen if America engaged in a process of truth and reconciliation, much like South Africa did? South Africa admitted its horrid racism; Germany admitted hers, but America has never admitted anything.

And perhaps that is, at least, part of the reason that the malady affecting white America is fear. There has been no resolution of the contradiction between American idealism (democracy) and American realism (separatism, racism, sexism, homophobia, Islamophobia). There has been no resolution of the conflict caused by the words "all men are created equal" and the specific American determination that black people:

1) Are not human, whether male or female; and

2) That they are not worthy of liberation, freedom, and basic human rights; and finally,

3) They are not being human, they are not "equal" to white people, nor can they ever be.

There has been no admitting of the fact that the 'Founding Fathers' did not include black people as those to be included in the dispensation of rights enumerated by and in the Constitution.

America has basked in the myth called "American Exceptionalism" which has as a core value the intent to keep some people out of the equation for liberty and justice.

DeGruy says that Americans have been able to exist with the contradictions presented by the Constitution because of something called "cognitive dissonance." That is, white Americans had to remove themselves from any thought of slavery being bad; they had to convince themselves that the treatment of black people by whites was not bad, but that the black people were bad and therefore deserved what they were getting.

But the holding onto the secret of the horrors of white racism has taken its toll on white people, says DeGruy, and has caused them to live in fear. So, at the end of the day, white supremacy has traumatized both black and white people. Black people are afraid of a government which has not and will not protect them; white people are afraid that perhaps their injustice, or complicity in the dispensation of injustice, will come back to haunt them.

DeGruy's theory is provocative, and it has merit. Untreated trauma is never a good thing; those who practice oppression have a fear that will not leave them that they will get what they have meted out. Thomas Jefferson, perhaps, puts into words the fear that many may feel:

"Indeed, I tremble for my country when I reflect that God is just; that His justice cannot sleep forever; that considering numbers, nature and natural means only, a revolution of the wheel of fortune, an exchange of situation, is among possible events; that it may become probably by supernatural influence!" (from Notes on the State of Virginia, Query XVIII: Manners)."

Robert Jensen goes further in Yes Magazine by saying, "Put bluntly: The United States abolished a formal apartheid system but remains a white-supremacist society." and again in the same article, "I have a choice: I can be white—that is, I can refuse to challenge white supremacy or centrality—or I can be a human being.

I can rest comfortably in the privileges that come with being white, or I can struggle to be fully human. But I can't do both. Though the work is difficult, the choice for those of us who are white should be easy."

This writer doesn't for one agree fully with both of the writers quoted above, for I do not think white supremacy is an American problem, but rather a problem of those who are of European or white descent in general that have not taken any form of responsibility for what their fore-fathers have done during slavery, but have benefited either directly or indirectly from what their fore-parents have accomplished and the so called progress or personal family gains they have made through slavery.

Of course there are exceptions to every rule, but the general pervasive behaviour of the European/ white supremacy apparatus is that blacks are inferior and are a threat to the social order of the subjugated versus the dominant Eurocentric society and therefore must be robustly controlled for economic and social reasons.

The popular myth that illustrates the white supremacy apparatus in action says that when Napoleon found out that the Sphinx was Egyptian and that Egyptians were black he ordered his soldiers to shoot off their flat noses.

This may or may not be true according to Tom Holmberg, *"One traveller to Egypt around the time of World War One wrote the following: "To take our photos sitting in front of the Sphinx on a camel was the aim of another. ...And so, repulsing the hordes of robbers on all sides, we came to the wonderful, inscrutable, worth-millions-of-pounds-to-authors Sphinx.*

The great riddle of the mysterious East. How many reams of rubbish have been written about this misshapen block of stone. Napoleon, a practical man, fired a few cannon balls at its face. High explosive shells were not invented in those days." [From: Sommers, Cecil. Temporary Crusaders. (London: John Lane, 1919) Chapter VI. "19th April." If you happen to be like me, you will notice it was a justification and not an explanation we just read.

Another book from about the same time called (In the Footsteps of Napoleon (1915) by James Morgan, p 85) states *"There is a tradition among the Arabs of the Pyramids that all the scars of time and the wounds of a hundred wars, which the Sphinx carries, were inflicted by Napoleon's soldiers, who used its mystifying and majestic countenance as a target.*

That, however, is only a legend for the tourist. Long before the discovery of gunpowder, the Arabs had laid iconoclastic hands on the beard of this god of the desert..." Though the Arab guides may have spread this tale, this myth has been perpetuated over the years by countless teachers the world over who have passed this bit of "history" on to their students.

A poll conducted on the Internet found that fully 21% of respondents believed Napoleon was responsible for the Sphinx's missing nose. One of the most recent examples of the persistence of this falsehood was Louis Farrakhan's "Million Man March" speech where he said: "White supremacy caused Napoleon to blow the nose off the Sphinx because it reminded you [sic] too much of the Black man's majesty."
And the perpetuation of this myth in "Afrocentric" circles was even the subject of a segment of the U.S. television investigative journalism program "60 Minutes."

Theodoros Karasavvas in his article, *"Why are Noses Missing from so Many Egyptian Statues?"* Poses three reasons which I have responded to in brackets:

1) Natural Erosion Has Played a Role (and it probably has happened to some extent).
2) Human Intervention is Definitely Another Major Factor (by this he means where white archaeologists have doctored the evidence and data they found in the black empires that they visited or have been dishonest

with the information, language, evidence or history that they found in the field).

3) Could it be Racism? (Bearing in mind that racism is the exercise of prejudice and power by the dominant group over the non-economically less powerful others of course it is a factor a very big factor as we shall see).

Karasavvas continues, *"According to some scholars, there was a deliberate attempt by early Egyptologists to deny and hide that Ancient Egypt was an African culture. According to the written account of Vivant Denon, a French artist, writer and archaeologist who etched the image of the Sphinx of Giza around 1798, the facial features of the famous monument appeared to be of African origin"* (This is shortly before the visit of Napoleon to Egypt between 1798-1801.

Now if Denon found the Sphinx alive and well so to speak in 1798 and Napoleon visited shortly after and the noses were missing, then Napoleon is the likely suspect with his hand caught in the cookie jar. This is why he has been cited as the likely suspect for the act of degradation, but of course we will never be sure).

However, this theory fails to explain why so many ancient Greek and Roman statues are also de-nosed and dismembered as well. Noses on the vast majority of ancient Greek and Roman stone sculptures are missing too. While some of these have inevitably broken off accidentally, it's pretty evident that an overwhelming number of them have been deliberately targeted.

Since it's historically, archaeologically and scientifically proven that the ancient Greeks and Romans were of European (Caucasian) origin, in this case racism wasn't likely to have been a reason for the intentional de-nosing of their statues."

In my humble estimation as the writer of this book, a denosing of statues of different racial origins with an overwhelming weight on those of African origin spells cover-up to me. For it is easy to hide the needle of crime in the haystack of general criminality and suffer but a few casualties in comparison of your own along the way and quietly accept those injuries, isn't it true? Of course!

If God is found to be black why do we need to call for the images to be changed back to their original colour? Why not just leave things as they are? The reason for this is that it simply perpetuates white supremacy and hides the truth about which all mankind should be concerned. For truth is important? If it was important yesterday, it's important today and if it's important today, it should always be important that we know the truth.

Not knowing the truth always alters the result, so the resulting outcomes should be and can only be based on whether something is a truth or a lie. Since the result you get is always based on the informational input you had to start with, truth leads to a truthful outcome and a lie leads you to a false conclusion that perpetuates lying and deception which is never a good thing.

Just as truth would matter if you were told that your mother and father were of a different colour to what they actually are today (changing the outcome – you expect). The truth about what colour or race God and the true Hebrews are including the truth behind what the Bible (the book of God says) affects those who look down on black people effects everyone.

It affects those who aspire to be white because they are looked down upon, those who have been living a lie thinking they are special or superior to others and those who are aware of the problems but despise the lies and want to know the truth.

I recently saw a black woman boldly walking around in public with her daughter's white doll displayed proudly in her hands in what could be interpreted as a vain display of ownership and I wanted to ask her why she had bought a white dolly for her black daughter. I avoided that temptation, however I had the thought that she clearly either subconsciously or ignorantly didn't understand that she was conditioning her young child to prefer white things and people over black ones.

She is in fact teaching her child to give deference to European things and people over African-Caribbean/ African American things and people. She is by her simple choice of toys, teaching her child that European is superior and preferred to black-African/ Caribbean as a brand.

I for one despise that lie. A lie that has been sold to black people for many years as colonial propaganda and it's time that it stopped, for Elohim created all men equal and none are superior to the other when it comes to people.

Quiz 2

1. What was the statement made by Megyn Kelly that set off the debate about the colour of Santa and Jesus (aka Yahoshuah?)

2. What was the real problem with her statement?

3. Why is God white in the first place and how did that affect the slaves?

4. What did the plantocracy do that kept the slaves in slavery for another 100 years?

5. Why are the noses missing from so many Egyptian statues?

6. Why should the images, paintings and statues be changed back to their original depictions?

7. What's wrong with black people giving their children white dollys?

8. Who is affected by the living out of a lie?

---

7. Everyone
6. Because truth matters
5. More than likely Napoleon shot them off
4. Manipulate slaves with the Bible
   situation of the oppressed.
3. He is the image of the oppressor and this justifies the
2. She stated it as a fact.
1. That both Santa and Jesus were definitely white.

Discussion

1. What are your observations about when everyone thought God was white?

2. How have attitudes changed now that some are challenging the status quo and saying that God is black?

3. Compare the response around God being white and God being black and what do you notice?

4. What is your position on the Colour of God at this time?

5. How possible that people are able to agree or disagree agreeably on their views about the colour of God?

6. What is the most important thing you will take away from this discussion?

7. How can we practically apply our conclusions about the importance of God being black or white?

CHAPTER 3
THE POPE KNOWS SOMETHING

In all the public worship services the Pope mostly worships a white Madonna and child such as the Sistine Madonna. *"Commissioned by Pope Julius II in 1513, and created by Raphael, The Sistine Madonna is one of the world's most recognizable paintings.*

Capturing the public's imagination ever since its creation, the two cherubs at the bottom of the altarpiece who sit as observers looking up at the Madonna and the Christ child as they descend from a heavenly space."

In most of the European Catholic Churches the likelihood is that all adherents will worship a white Madonna (A Madonna made in the image of the Europeans). In fact it's no different around the world except at a few sites.

Mary is likely to be white European and so too is the likelihood of the priesthood being mostly white European, especially at the top (which we shall come to later). However, the worship of a black Madonna is actually more prevalent in Europe than anywhere else in the world and this is a mystery that is probably not connected to Mary but to something much more ancient.

In the article Christian mystery schools, cults and heresies, it says, *"Other researchers into the mystique of the Black Madonna state that the reasons that the Roman Catholic Church in general has not warmly embraced such depictions of the Holy Mother or Virgin Mary are because they fear that such representations are actually paying tribute to the ancient goddesses and Earth mothers and that these images perpetuate strains of pagan worship of the female principle.*

For example, church scholars point out that St. Germain de Pres, the oldest church in Paris (Par-isis, the Grove of Isis), was built in 542 on the site of a former temple dedicated to Isis.

Isis had been the patron goddess of Paris until Christianity replaced her with St. Genevieve. Within the church of St. Germain de Pres, however, parishioners worshipped a black statue of Isis until it was destroyed in 1514.

Christianity warred against goddess worship from the days of the apostles when St. Paul (d. 62-68 C.E.) found to his great frustration that his message was being shouted down by the crowds at Ephesus who pledged their obeisance to Diana. Until they had been modernized and westernized, Diana/Artemis, together with the other two preeminent goddesses of the East, Isis and Cybele, who were first represented as black Madonnas.

And before the people of the East bent their knees to Diana, Isis, and Cybele, they had worshipped the Great Mother as Inanna in Sumeria, as Ishtar in Babylonia, and as Astarte among the Hebrews. Most scholars agree that among the first images of the Black Madonna and her son were representations of Isis and Horus"

According to the website article, *"The black Madonna in Europe"* The Black Madonnas originally all had African features before most of them were destroyed by iconoclasts (people who were against icons). When they were replaced, the artists retained the dark skin colour, but not being familiar with the image of real Africans, they gave their European features to the paintings and images.

In cases where originals have survived, you are likely to witness African features on Mary and her child Jesus, cases such as the Black Madonna of Nuria, Spain – called *"The Queen of the Pyrenees. And Russia's remarkable legacy of Black Madonnas and other Christian icons of a dark skin is evidenced in the book, Russian Icons by Vladimir Ivanov, including the feature story of the Spring 1994 issue of Russian Life magazine, graced with a Black Madonna on its cover."*

By examining the abundant evidence available, we can see that what history shows is different from what we see happening in the Catholic Church today. What it exposes is that there has been a mother-baby cult long before a Mary cult ever existed and that this false worship system that began in Babylon in ancient times then spread to Egypt and to the Bible lands under many names is older than the Catholic Church and its daughters.

We actually find that the Roman Empire picked up the idea of mother-baby worship from the heathens they conquered and used the Catholic Church to make this legacy of a black mother goddess universal initially as the black Madonna who later morphs into the form of Mary. We also find that Mary is later changed from being black to being European and that this white Mary is what has been taught and perpetuated amongst the nations of the world where the Catholic Church has brought its brand of Christianity in order to prop up 'white supremacy.'

Having said that the Popes both past and present have always worshipped in private before a different image of Mary from the one that they pray to in public. In public, they worship before a white European looking Mary most of the time, but in private the Pope prays to a black Madonna and appear to be especially partial to the black Madonna of Poland according to popular news (check it out for yourself).

It is still however noticeable that the Madonna and her baby Jesus are both black (Semitic) people and always have been until the European Church decided to change that image to one that they felt represented them visually and with which they were more comfortable as a minority group on planet earth.

It was not a happy moment when they realised that the visual representation of the majority of humans on the planet were of a black skin and that the people group to which the Europeans belonged were actually a minority group of this planet. They came along and found the images, idols and false and true God already here. They decided to change that because in their minds, God could not and should not be a black man.

What does the Pope know? From an article, "The real Jesus by John R. Moore we read, *"Cesare Borgia , a homosexual and mass murderer who was used as the model for the long blonde haired, blue eyed effeminate looking Christ, which Christians the world over have been bowing down to and worshipping for centuries.*

It was during the Renaissance period after contact was made with Africa, that the Dark Ages in Europe came to an end and paintings began to circulate portraying Mary and Jesus with white skin, blue eyes and blond hair. Many of the later paintings of Jesus Christ were based on Cesare Borgia, which in turn have influenced the majority of the portraits of Christ created from that point onwards.

History bears witness to the millions killed for not worshipping the false image of Christ. Rome and Spain dispatched the likes of Christopher Columbus, Hernan Cortes, Ponce De Leon, Arnericus Vespucci among others with armies to kill, enslave and also indoctrinate Blacks and native Indians into Christianity.

When Altobello Melone painted his portrait of Christ around 1520, he drew inspiration from an earlier Cesare Borgia painting, but distorted the distinctions between the faces and ethnicities of the most holy figure with one of the most corrupt."

The website, 'Isrealite.net' goes on to say, *"The images and idols displayed in the churches are not of Christ. Michelangelo first painted the most common religious image used in deceiving the world today.*

It is a picture of a blue-eyes European with blond hair, who they maliciously claim to be Jesus Christ. This false image was modelled after Cesare Borgia, who was the second son of so-called Pope Alexander VI, of Rome. The real Jesus, according to all scientific and historical facts, is an Afro-Asiatic man."

I don't know about the Asiatic bit, but I'm absolutely sure that He could not have been white European. That is an impossibility that has been a prevalent lie for centuries and it has been told so long that even the fraudsters believe it. The truth is that God is a black man. He may be Asiatic black, He may be Hamitic looking black, but one thing is for sure, He was and is a Semitic black man.

The truth is out then, the Pope knows that Yahoshuah was a black man and has continued the great tradition of continuing the façade that a Semitic black man is actually European in appearance. This is a lie that has been perpetuated without cause or foundation and no other reason can be found for the continuation of the lie other than racism. Though some would contend that this tradition exceeds Cesare Borgia, the fact is that it's not about Borgia but it about truth being honored and restored to the public domain. In other words, everyone should know the truth.

Quiz 3

1. What kind of statue is the Sistine Madonna?

2. What is the most likely colour of most Madonna statues?

3. Who is said to have been the patron goddess of Paris?

4. What colour were the first representations of these goddesses?

5. What racial features did the original black Madonnas have?

6. Who picked up the idea of mother-child worship and how has it been used?

7. Who have the Popes past and present worshipped in private?

8. Who was Cesare Borgia?

1. A White Madonna
2. White
3. Isis
4. Black
5. Negroid
6. The Catholic Church, used for control
7. Black Madonnas and Jesus,
8. A gangster.

Discussion

1. What have you understood from this lesson that the Popes have known all along?

2. When you look at the issue of the Catholic Church knowing information that they withheld how do you feel?

3. What would you say or ask the Pope if he was in front of you right now?

4. Compare the black Madonnas and the White Madonnas and what are your thoughts?

5. What stands out for you about the origin of the trinity, the Madonnas and what the Pope knows that has him praying in private to a black Madonna?

6. How can you apply this knowledge practically to your walk with Elohim?

CHAPTER 4
THE EASTERN ORTHODOX CHURCH
KNOWS SOMETHING TOO

The Eastern Orthodox Church is the eastern branch of the Catholic Church and has exercised greater honesty by more publically acknowledging the history and presence of a black Madonna and baby Messiah from the every off-set. Such evidence is quite plentiful as presented by the book, "Russian Icons."

It should be publicly acknowledged that in an article about if Catholics worship images and statues it says, *"Non-Catholic religions of today considered the Catholic practice of giving homage, respect, honour or reverence to God, to the Blessed Virgin Mary or to Saints through the use of Images or statue resembling God and His heavenly creatures as a literal worshiping of these pictures, images, statue or icons itself per se. It is similar to putting words into the mouth of the* Catholics.

Every country have statues and pictures or bursts of iconic persons like ex-presidents, national heroes and many more but their paying homage to whom it represents is not considered worshiping nor idolizing. To everyone this is normal to remember special people who ones lived."

Many of these versions of Mary can be seen on the Interfaith Mary page by Ella Rozett. However what the writer of the article above fails to recognise is that in the Catholic Church these images, statues etc have been designed with the explicit purpose of being used for worship. This is not the case with other statues of the famous or heroes in general.

In the article, Eastern orthodox icons the writer says, *"By the sixth century, Christian buildings were full of icons placed on walls, ceilings, floors, and in shrines. During the eighth and ninth centuries, they became the subject of a violent controversy.*

The Iconoclastic Controversy, which raged for more than one hundred years (730-843), began with the temporary victory of the image destroyers ("iconoclasts"), who believed that icons were closer to idolatry than true worship and that the image of the human form could not embody spiritual presence.

In 730, an imperial edict banned religious imagery throughout the Byzantine Empire, and artists were either forced to migrate to the west or to turn their talents to secular subjects. The ban was lifted in 843 and religious painting was again encouraged in Byzantium.

Icon painting, particularly in Russia and Greece, has continued to flourish for centuries, extending the life of the style well beyond the collapse of the Byzantine Empire in 1453. In use, the panels are quickly blackened by incense and smoke from the devotional candles that burn before them, and therefore many have been frequently repainted. The repainting retains, however, the basic forms."

What has changed in recent years is neither the iconography or image worship of the Catholic or Orthodox Church but rather the complex cover up that has happened and continues to be encouraged in an increasingly information driven age that allows important facts to be discovered and acknowledged more widely than perhaps ever before. It is hard for information to remain hidden that can be researched, checked, verified and shared all over the world almost instantly, and what is happening is exactly that.

Now God (Elohim) has not changed. He has remained the same, He has left the truth to be discovered by those who want to ask, seek and knock until the information is available. Both Mary and Jesus (so called) have always been black and nothing has changed about that, they are still black, but there has been a conscious conspiracy to change the truth because it's inconvenient for the dominant few that Yahoshuah should be black and that the subjugated many should find this truth out and use it against the dominant few.

The Detroit Baptist seminary website says, *"Although Roman Catholicism and Eastern Orthodoxy are different in a number of ways—some superficial and some substantial, they both set up human priests (and saints) as intermediaries between God and humans. They both encourage the use of images (whether icons or statues) as aids to worship and prayer. And both see their respective Churches as fulfilling the role of authoritative interpreter of Scripture.*

More anecdotally, they both seem to encourage a great deal of religious ritualism and activity but very little actual study of the Bible. "The difference between what the Western and Eastern orthodox church practice in terms of worship is seen by their use of statues and icons (pictures) to facilitate worship. "Another thing one is quickly struck with when walking into an Orthodox church is the pervasive presence and use of icons. In some cases, the beauty of such icons is awe-inspiring, and in fact, that seems to be the point.

However, the icons in an Orthodox church are usually quite different from those found in Roman Catholic churches. Whereas Catholic churches often include statues and carved or otherwise 3-dimensionally shaped crucifixes, within the Orthodox tradition religious imagery is carefully controlled and for the most part is produced on a flat surface using paint or something similar.

As in Roman Catholicism, within Orthodoxy icons are viewed as means that can assist people in their worship. Both traditions make use of images or icons as aids to worship. And so, church goers in both traditions often venerate and pray to images of Jesus as well the apostles and other saints. Both church traditions also make use of relics for similar purposes."

It is noticeable that Icons tend to be the favoured mode of facilitating worship in the Eastern Orthodox Church, while in the west the favoured mode is that of statues and carvings. These inducements to false worship are all in contravention to the direct command of Elohim:

In **Exodus 20:3-6,** "Thou shalt have no other gods before me. Thou shalt not make unto thee any graven image, or any likeness of anything that is in heaven above, or that is in the earth beneath, or that is in the water under the earth: thou shalt not bow down thyself to them, nor serve them: for I the Lord thy God am a jealous God, visiting the iniquity of the father upon the children unto the third and fourth generation of them that hate me; and showing mercy unto thousands of them that love me, and keep my commandments."

What both the Eastern and Western Catholic church doesn't appear to know is that idolatry or worship of anything but the one and only true Elohim angers Him. What they appear to have forgotten is that a prohibition to represent Elohim by any image in heaven or earth has been issued. They have forgotten that any image of Yahoshuah either true or false is also prohibited. Thus images of any form representing Yahoshuah are forbidden and at best they are a lie but at worst they are idolatry that Elohim will sooner or later judge.

Both traditions have set themselves up with human priests and iconised or carved images as intermediaries between man and Elohim, but there is but one mediator between man and Elohim and that is Yahoshuah the Man-God through whom we pray to the Father and receive answers to our prayers. <u>1 Timothy 2:5</u>, *"For there is one God and one mediator between God and men, the man Christ Jesus;"*

Yahoshuah is the only intermediary between Elohim and His creation. Mary cannot stand between God and man, Saints cannot stand between God and his creatures and neither can priests. Elohim has created one to die for the sins of the whole world and His name is Yahoshuah. It is He and He alone who has been given the task of mediation.

Quiz 4

1. What has the Eastern Orthodox exercised more than the Catholic Church?

2. What kind of Church buildings are full of statues and fetishes?

3. What kind of Church buildings are likely to be filled with icons?

4. What do both Catholics and Eastern Orthodoxy have in common?

5. What do both branches of Catholicism encourage?

6. What excuse do they give for using statues and icons?

7. What is the favoured mode of worship in the Eastern Orthodox Church?

7. What is Elohim's view about spiritual mediation?

1. Honesty
2. Catholic Churches and her daughter churches
3. Easter Orthodox ones
4. Idolatry
5. The setting up of intermediaries
6. It facilitates worship
7. Icons
8. Only Yahoshuah is a qualified mediator between God and men.

Discussion

1. What do you see in the Eastern Orthodox Church that immediately catches your eyes when you walk in?

2. How do you define the word 'icon?'

3. What is different when you compare the Catholic and Orthodox Church traditions and what is similar?

4. What stands out in this lesson as impacting for you most?

5. What key lesson would you say you can apply to your life based on this discussion?

CHAPTER 5
WHEN WAS GOD EVER WHITE EUROPEAN?

The website of the American Bible society in an article on 'Blacks in Bible antiquity' says, *"The view of Africa that has evolved in recent centuries has little or no historical integrity inasmuch as it reflects Eurocentric interpretations of the Bible.*

However, new light is shining on biblical antiquity, and layers of unfavourable biases are being peeled away. In their place is a more congenial basis for inclusiveness and reconciliation in conjunction with an emergence of critical studies on the Black presence in the Bible and the recovering of ancient African heritage in the Scriptures.

Consequently, persons of African descent now have the opportunity to rediscover consistent and favourable mentioning of their forebears within the pages of the Bible."

Historically it was never possible for Yahoshuah to ever be white due to the area of the globe that he originated from. Neither were His apostles ever likely to be white, nor even the Hebrews in general ever white. So there is no validity to a white Mary, a white Jesus (Yahoshuah) white apostles and disciples or even white European Jews.

In a Huffpost article by Taryn Finley entitled, "Jesus wasn't white and here's why that matters?" she says "It wasn't until the Middle Ages when artists began depicting Jesus as white because Christians didn't like the idea of Jesus having Jewish features, even though he was Jewish. Ramsey also said that many speculate that Biblical passages that referred to lightness symbolizing purity and darkness symbolizing sin and evil played into how people perceived Jesus' appearance.

Again, we see this narrative of dark skin people being bad, thus needing to be tamed or killed in order to conform to the good, or white, standard," Ramsey said. She touches on the notion of white supremacy being used in Christianity to colonize and control before and during slavery. Despite white people using Christianity to justify their wrongdoings, black people found their own way of practicing it to seek liberation.

Historically, the white Jesus has been used to oppress and erase the histories of people of color in a way that Korean Jesus or black Jesus has not. Franchesca Ramsey's point isn't that Christianity is bad because it's been misused to oppress. But rather that white power structures excluded images of Jesus as he really was, with a darker complexion in order to spread racial bias.

"While a Korean or a black Jesus might not be historically accurate (I believe a black Yahoshuah is) — just like a blonde-haired, blue-eyed Jesus — people of color have the right to see themselves in their religion, especially after centuries of being taught and forced to worship a God that doesn't look like them."

She continues, *"While Jesus' true facial features may remain a mystery, it should be obvious that using religion to covertly justify discrimination is fundamentally hypocritical."*

While His facial features or exact likeness are a mystery, His colour is not: He was historically and factually black. Biblically none of the major figures of the Bible were ever white.

In fact the only person mentioned as white as snow was the leprosy stricken servant of Elisha who was "Ghazi" (recorded in **2 Kings 5:27**). Everyone else was definitely and absolutely black. But sometimes Christianity can seem like a white man's religion because of the lies that have been told to reinforce and preserve this lie.

Even modern articles like those found on the website, 'Gotquestions.org' tell a skewed story that twists the facts and misleads the readers. In it, in answer to the question, "Is Christianity a white man's religion?"

The writer states as if it is a fact, *"In the past 2,000 years, the vast majority of Christians have been white/European. While Christianity had its beginnings in the Middle East, it spread rapidly to Europe and parts of Asia where Caucasians were the predominant race.*

The history of Christianity is filled with expansions, but mostly throughout Europe and Asia, then on to the West in the 15th century. Christianity has not had nearly the same success spreading among Middle Easterners, Africans, and Asians, and this has led many to declare that Christianity is a religion for white people.

Christianity was never intended for white people only. The first Christians were all Semitic in ethnicity and likely had light- to dark-brown skin. Christianity having been predominantly a white religion in past centuries has nothing to do with the message of Christianity.

*Rather, it is due to the failure of Christians to take the Gospel of Jesus Christ to the ends of the world (**Matthew 28:19-20; Acts 1:8**). The apostle John declared that Jesus Christ is the propitiation for the sins of the entire world [all races and nationalities] (see **1 John 2:2**).*

*Spiritually, men of all races are one due to the presence of a common sickness—sin. Sin entered the human race at the fall, and because of Adam and Eve's disobedience, sin has been an inheritance for all of their descendants. **Romans 5:12** tells us that, through Adam, sin entered the world and so death was passed on to all men because all have sinned.*

*But just as sin entered the human race by one man, so does redemption come by one Man, Jesus Christ. Forgiveness of sin, the essence of Christianity, is offered to all races, colors, creeds, and genders, to all "those who receive God's abundant provision of grace and of the gift of righteousness" through Him (**Romans 5:18**).*

*In giving His life as a substitute for sin, Jesus Christ purchased for God with His blood "men from every tribe and tongue and people and nation" (**Revelation 5:9**). No, Christianity is not a white man's religion. Christianity is not a black, brown, red, or yellow religion either. The truth of the Christian faith is universally applicable to all people."*

The article makes several claims with which I cannot agree. The first is that over the past 2000 years the majority of people who were Christians were white Europeans. This is impossible since Christianity originated in North East Africa so that the first Christians would have been black and so would the first converts and those who came before the faith went west to Europe. These for the most part were Africans like the Ethiopian Eunuch of Acts Chapter 8.

Secondly the white Europeans were and still are a minority in the world today representing at best 15% or the world's population and most of them are not believers but at best agnostics. The majority of believers today are still persons of colour. Thirdly the writer is correct when s/he writes that Christianity was never meant to be a white man's religion because it was actually a subset of the Hebrew Faith. The correct way to say what he said is; "Christianity was never meant to be the religion of only the black man or true Hebrew it was intended for the whole world."

However it is at the point of contact with the Europeans that the Gospel has become polluted and subverted by the Roman Catholic Church and the Jewish people who have adopted or adapted it as the state religion of the Europeans. As a result the faith was misused and manipulated as a tool of oppression for Europeans (which so called Jewish people really are) used against true Hebrews and as a result slavery was allowed to be justified using the Bible.

It is inaccurate to say that Christianity has no colour however because it is and was the religion of the Hebrew and Hebrews are persons of colour. It is just that now the Faith is to be shared with all men, but make no mistake it has a colour and the colour is black because both Elohim and His people are black.

Archeologically none of the nations in the so called, 'Middle East' were ever white nations. Not the Arabs (mixed and mingled people) who live around the Hebrews, nor the nations surrounding them either. For these nations were either Semitic or Hamitic in origin and nature. The Japhethite (Europeans) races were much further abroad in the colder countries of Europe until very recently. So the archaeological evidence is in favour of the black people whether it's from Babylon to Timbuktu.

Ethnographically (by people group) all black people are not the same. As it has already been proven through Zondervan dictionary. The Africans come from Ham but there are another group of black people that do not. Zondervan Bible Dictionary: Says of Ham: *"The youngest son of Noah born probably about 96 years before the Flood; and one of eight persons to live through the Flood. He became the progenitor of the dark races; **not the Negroes**, but the Egyptians, Ethiopians, Libyans and Canaanites."*

Noticed the statement, **"not the Negroes"**. The question then becomes, who are the Negroes if they are not descended from Ham? The Negroes are actually from the line of Noah's son Shem. Negros are Shemites and Shemites are Negros. They are one and the same and they were historically black people.

Semitic people are of the line of Abraham, Isaac, Jacob and the 12 sons of Jacob who are also known as the Children of Israel. These are the true Hebrew Israelites of the Torah/bible. So No! All black people may be black on the outside, but some are Hamitic and some a Shemetic (Semitic) in origin and are therefore not the same except for their colour.

Every ethnic group knows what specific country or history they have connected with them as a people except the so called, 'Negro.' My research into being a Hebrew has led me to believe that most 'Negros' are the scattered Israelites who had their country, language, culture and nationality stolen from them by Europeans. The jealousy of the Romans led them to the point where they white washed our land and our culture and Elohim having stripped even our faith from us and sought to transform us into Gentiles and them into Jews **(Psalm 83:2-8)**.

Though the Japhathite European Jewish people make a claim to be Jewish, they are actually not and for this I will give a few reasons:

1. Their lifestyle is incompatible with scripture in that they reject Yahoshuah as their Messiah and reject the Covenant also and yet are doing extremely well economically owning much of the music industry, much property and worldly wealth. In his series on the Hip Hop industry, Minster G. Craig Lewis exposes the Ashkenazi ownership of the record industry (Via Universal, Sony and Waner) which companies could be said to have been responsible for the weaponisation of the music industry.

2. They have the star of Ramphan (Satan) as their national flag (**Acts 7:43 and Amos 5:26**). They say it is the Star of David or of Solomon, but nowhere in the scripture does it even suggest either. You cannot find it because it's not there in the Bible. The only link that can be found to this pentagram is its usage in conjuring up demon spirits as ascribed to it by witches and warlocks.

3. Next is the DNA evidence which you can research yourself on Google that clearly tells the secret identity of the Jewish people as Khazar-Japhethite-European people of a Turkic origin that are pretending to Semitic when they are really Japhetic (read about this in my book, "Black skin royal identity").

4. Finally the Bible exposes them in **Revelations 2:9 and 3:9** by saying, *"Who say that they are Jews but are not!"* You can't get clearer than that can you? If the Bible which is a prophetic book of the Hebrews speaks about them before they ever even knew what they were doing and accurately exposes their tactics, we should listen and take it on board that they are, **'not the true Jews'**.

Economically yes the so called 'Jewish' have been able to make the Hebrew faith seem like a white man's religion! There is no doubt that their dominant economic power has tipped the balance in modern times as the Jewish people, and they have become richer than any other people as a group.

The richest family in the world is the Rothschild family (who are Zionists) and the rest of the Jewish people as a whole either own or control the assets of the world not controlled by that family through the banking system, politicians, the media, the film industry, insurance, music and publishing. This effectively means that the world is run by the so called Jews or their proxies because money answers every matter and they have and control the money (**Ecclesiastes 10:19**).

Quiz 5

1. How true is the view of Africa written about in recent centuries?

2. What is being peeled away by recent research?

3. What kind of mentioning have we now started to find concerning persons of African descent?

4. What is one of the factors that makes it impossible historically for Yahoshuah to have been a white man?

5. How has the theory of the white God been used?

6. Can you think of any figure of the Bible mentioned as white?

7. How have white writers tried to justify a white God?

Discussion

1. What have you notice about how the theory of a white God is used?

2. When people say that God is not black, what colour do they usually ascribe to Him and why?

3. Why is the colour or ethnicity of God important or not important?

4. Compare the argument that God is black versus the one that says He is white and which do you think carries the burden of proof and why?

5. How will the conclusion about the Colour of Yahoshuah being black benefit persons of Colour?

6. How does the same conclusion benefit persons who are not of colour?

7. What one thing will you take away from this discussion and how will you use it?

CHAPTER 6
WHY DID GOD CHOOSE TO BE BLACK

Elohim chose Israel knowing that they were the least of all nations and not because they were the best or strongest of nations. **Deuteronomy 7:7-9** tells us, *"The LORD did not set His affection on you and choose you because you were more numerous than other peoples, for you were the fewest of all peoples.*

But it was because the LORD loved you and kept the oath He swore to your forefathers that He brought you out with a mighty hand and redeemed you from the land of slavery, from the power of Pharaoh king of Egypt. Know therefore that the LORD your God is God; He is the faithful God, keeping His covenant of love to a thousand generations of those who love Him and keep His commands."

Yahoshuah had to come from some nation or people, and Elohim sovereignly chose Israel. He made a promise to Abraham, Isaac and Jacob for His Word could only be fulfilled through the medium of Messiah the promised seed.

When Elohim chose them, they were a nation of slaves and despised by the Egyptians. They were looked down upon by other nations because they didn't have a King, or an army, or even a land, or great riches to boast of. They were wanderers, without a homeland, without castles, fortresses, farms or even houses to live in.

The website, 'Got questions.org' says, *"However, God's reason for choosing the nation of Israel was not solely for the purpose of producing the Messiah. God's desire for Israel was that they would go and teach others about Him. Israel was to be a nation of priests, prophets, and missionaries to the world.*

God's intent was for Israel to be a distinct people, a nation who pointed others towards God and His promised provision of a Redeemer, Messiah, and Saviour. For the most part, Israel failed in this task. However, God's ultimate purpose for Israel — that of bringing the Messiah into the world — was fulfilled perfectly in the Person of Jesus Christ."

So Elohim knew we would be looked down upon and be overlooked by the nations. He had a mission for a people to be special, different from what the nations had been and He desired a people who would work in partnership with Him to spread the message of the Messiah who is the deliverer of the whole Earth.

We as a people were to declare the reality of Elohim by our words as prophetic evangelists, our lifestyles of separation from sin as partners, and our life message of holiness through our examples as the mercy, grace and favour of Elohim to us was being worked out in us for all to see.

He had chosen us not because He had to, but because He could and wanted to. It needs to be clearly understood that Elohim is a sovereign God who is in charge of the world and even the entire universe. He makes His own decisions independent of any human interference or control. He is the Master of the universe and every dimension that there is, He is sovereign Lord.

So let me tell you the story of King David to illustrate a point. The king found out that it is only when you are dethroned or ordinary that you really find out who loves you and who is against you. At one time during his reign, King David was kicked out, disposed and stripped of his kingly majesty and it was then that he found out the truth that lived in the hearts of some of his people.

At this stage of his life, he met two men; one cursed him and told him exactly how he felt about him. The man let him know that he did not consider him to have been his king but rather had wished him the very worst in the past, present and future. King David's response was basically that God was at work. The truth is that Elohim was at work revealing the heart of the man to David so that if He ever restored the King, David would know where the man's loyalties lay. Isn't it good to know who is for you and who is against you?

During the same period, David met another man that loved him even though he had never met him before. This man was old but was willing to give up (sacrifice) his comfort to be with David. He fed and provided for David during his time of banishment from his kingdom.

He did everything he could to help and support. When asked about reward the man wanted nothing except that, should David ever get back into power that he should bless this man's descendants and treat them good in his stead.

This was the story of Shimei (**2 Samuel 16:5-13**) and Barzillai (**2 Samuel 17:27-29 and 19:31-40**) both of whom met David during his banishment and had two different responses to the plight of the King. I tell these stories to illustrate that it's not when you are in your position of strength and authority that others will show their true colours but rather when you are in a position of weakness and when you are down-and-out.

These stories demonstrate adequately what has happened to our Elohim and His people. He has come down as a black man by divine decision to see how Jews and Gentiles would treat Him and we crucified Him. We treated Him badly and then did the same to His people.

He came down as a black man and made His people black and the whole world has turned against them all. The true Hebrews have been rejected, subjugated, distressed, enslaved and abused. We have been the lowest of the low because of breaking Elohim's covenant we have been mistreated both because we are His people and because we have sinned against Him.

However woe be it unto the people and nation who have done this deed for there is a universal law of sowing and reaping that must be answered; so their time is coming too, a time when they must be enslaved a time when they will be made low a time of divined judgement just as Shimei was judged by David so must all the nations that profited from the slavery of Yah's people be judged by the true King of Kings.

Elohim unlike David chose His situation in order to prove the nations. Through the opportunity to do evil or good, the hearts of the people of the nations would be revealed. They would have both the opportunity and the power to choose how to treat His people.

When they had the upper hand and His people were at their lowest point just as in the situation of David. We find out through our recorded history that the nations chose to enslave them, treat them evilly and to take advantage of them. This will not be forgotten by a living and just Elohim, what they have sown, they shall surely reap.

Our decisions don't affect the decisions Elohim makes. Nor does it mean that Elohim is not free to make His own decision either in line with or contrary to the decisions that men make as sovereign individuals. Elohim has given man free will but also reserves the right and power to make His own decisions independently also.

We can but do the right or wrong thing and reap the benefits or consequences of those decisions that we make. The day of consequences are coming to the nations. For they have failed their trial just as the Hebrews did and if Elohim judged us for the breaking of His covenant, what will be the judgement of those that have taken advantage of our downfall?

Elohim fore-knew that black people would be despised by the world. In scripture He foretells what Yahoshuah would be like in **Isaiah 53:3**, *"He is despised and rejected of men; a man of sorrows, and acquainted with grief: and we hid as it were our faces from him; he was despised, and we esteemed him not."*

The scripture continues in **Verse 7**, *"He was oppressed, and he was afflicted, yet he opened not his mouth: he is brought as a lamb to the slaughter, and as a sheep before her shearers is dumb, so he openeth not his mouth."*

Elohim foreknew that His people were a cursed people. For it is He that made covenant with us and set down the conditions as written in **Deuteronomy 28:15**, *"But it shall come to pass, if thou wilt not hearken unto the voice of the Lord thy God, to observe to do all his commandments and his statutes which I command thee this day; that all these curses shall come upon thee, and overtake thee:"*

Our Elohim knew that we would not just be despised, but that we would as a result of the curse be a rejected people because of the curse that was over us as a nation. **Deuteronomy 28:37**, *"And thou shalt become an astonishment, a proverb, and a byword, among all nations whither the Lord shall lead thee."*

And again, In **Deuteronomy 28:43-45**, *"The stranger that is within thee shall get up above thee very high; and thou shalt come down very low. He shall lend to thee, and thou shalt not lend to him: he shall be the head, and thou shalt be the tail. Moreover all these curses shall come upon thee, and shall pursue thee, and overtake thee, till thou be destroyed; because thou hearkenedst not unto the voice of the Lord thy God, to keep his commandments and his statutes which he commanded thee."*

The people would become a nation of slaves and servants because of the curse and our Messiah would share in our curse by becoming a servant also. **Isaiah 42:1-4**, *"Behold my servant, whom I uphold; mine elect, in whom my soul delighteth; I have put my spirit upon him: he shall bring forth judgment to the Gentiles.*

He shall not cry, nor lift up, nor cause his voice to be heard in the street. A bruised reed shall he not break, and the smoking flax shall he not quench: he shall bring forth judgment unto truth. He shall not fail nor be discouraged, till he have set judgment in the earth: and the isles shall wait for his law."

Our Messiah was humble according to the book of **Philippians 2:5-8**, *"Let this mind be in you, which was also in Christ Jesus: Who, being in the form of God, thought it not robbery to be equal with God: But made himself of no reputation, and took upon him the form of a servant, and was made in the likeness of men: And being found in fashion as a man, he humbled himself, and became obedient unto death, even the death of the cross."*

Elohim chose to be black because the deck is stacked against the black person in this world. There is an impediment upon the lives of the black people that must be recognised and there is something that everyone can do about it. Isaac Adams wrote an article on the website '9Marks.org' about the topic of *'Why white churches are hard for black people'*. In it he makes about thirteen points that I want to reiterate.

1. Many people of other races have not fought against racism because it does not directly affect them or their families.
2. Lots of white people have privileges that blacks don't.
3. It feels like the majority doesn't want to hear what it feels like to be black.
4. They think they are a safe space for blacks, but it's really not so.
5. Many people do not understand the experience of black people whether corporate or individual.
6. Sometimes blacks are made to feel like projects instead of peers.
7. "Gospel-unity" should mean togetherness but often means being an exception
8. Blacks are often only seen as the "other." Some outsider rather than part of the family,
9. The hall of faith seems somewhat white washed.

10. Black sisters and brothers are seen as second-class to marry.
11. All-white leadership doesn't promote blacks in some white churches.
12. It's easy to be black and lonely in a white church because no one wants to be a real friend with all of its investments.
13. When some white people call for "dying to yourself," they in effect mean, "assimilate or leave."

"Whether black or white, we are CHRISTIANS OR HEBREW APOSTOLICS — which means we should not give up on one another because God (Elohim) in Christ has never given up on us. Perhaps you're wondering what to do now having read this part of the book. On this long mile, here are a few places you can start:

a) Pray regularly for the eyes of your understanding to be opened wider on these issues.

b) Pray regularly for those of other ethnicities to understand and accept our identity.

c) Pray regularly to be sensitive for opportunities to love those that are unlike you so they can by your example learn to love and celebrate the differences as well as the similarities.

d) Pray for the unity of the Hebrew and true apostolic people all over the world as they awaken to who they really are"

Quiz 6

1. Where was Israel on the table of nations when Elohim chose them?

2. What was Elohim's main reason for choosing the nation of Israel?

3. Why did Elohim choose the Hebrews to be His people?

4. What story explains when you know who really loves you?

5. What did Elohim foreknow about His people?

6. What did our Messiah do through the incarnation?

7. What has Elohim on Christ demonstrated that He will never do?

---

7. Forsake His people
6. Identify with His people's pain
5. That they would be despised
4. The story of David
3. Because He could
2. To bring Messiah into the world
1. The least of all nations

Discussion

1. What are your observations about the behaviour of others when they have the upper hand?

2. How do you behave when you discover you have the upper hand, truthfully?

3. Compare the behaviour of the nations with the way that Elohim has treated us all and what do you discover?

4. How will the way that the nations have treated the true Hebrews work against them in the future?

5. What lessons can we learn from this discussion?

6. What will you do differently in life so that the law of sowing and reaping works for you and not against you from this point forward?

CHAPTER 7
FROM WHERE DOES THE WHITE MAN COME

What has been forgotten by those who have descended from the black man is: 'Honour rather than despise your father and your mother.' If as the theory goes that the oldest remains ever found of a human being are of a black person, then that means everyone is descended from black people, right?

The bible defines the first hu-man (man of colour) as a coloured man (Adam) based on the materials out of which he was created or formed. *"And the LORD God formed man of the **dust of the ground**, and breathed into his nostrils the breath of life; and man became a living soul"* **Genesis 2:7**.

If the dust of the earth (meaning the soil) is a dark-brown colour and God formed man from this substance, it is more than likely that the first man would be a man of colour that is somewhere between reddish brown and a rich dark brown or so called black. Go look at the colour of your dirt outside you home again and you will see what I'm talking about.

The main focus of this chapter is to take a look at where Europeans came from based on the work of specific scientists and ethnographers. So my first question is: Are whites the albino offspring of Black Africans? Because so called, 'white skin' is actually a form of albinism. It appears that whites have "come into being" through a number of possible pathways: In the Isis Papers p123, Dr. Frances Cress Welsing states *"Whites are undoubtedly a genetic mutant albino population... from the original Black (hue-man) beings."*

That is to say, she believes that white Europeans are a mutation of the man of colour or the black man.

The story of 'Snowflake' the albino gorilla dramatically illustrates how it is possible for white Europeans to come into being from blacks: Born of coal black parents, this albino gorilla named "Snowflake" has platinum blond hair, white (pink) skin, and blue eyes! (National Geographic: Mar. 67, Oct. 70). Similarly in Panama, particularly among the San Blas Indians who are albino natives they also have blond hair and blue eyes!

So we have been able to find about four different theories for the development of the white (Caucasoid race.) none of which are particularly flattering.

1. The mutation albino theory (Dr Frances Cress Welsing).

2. The leprosy theory - The Bible refers to white skin as leprosy (Num. 12:10-12, Lev. 13) and reports that a race of people (Gahazites) was born white due to being cursed! (II Kings 5:27).

3. The Japhethite settlement theory - Bible scholars credit Japheth (a son of Noah) as fathering a (Black) people who settled in the north country, ultimately becoming the Caucasian Race (a mysterious how?)

4. The gradual lightening of the Africans theory - Some scholars theorize that Africans who migrated to Europe and were caught in the Ice Age, gradually lightened until their genes

mutated to adapt to the scant sunlight, thus producing a race of white (pink skinned people).

Of all the four theories, there is a great amount of apparent understandable merit to the mutation theory which has been studied and put forward by the late Dr Cress-Welsing using mutated white mice to evidence her theory of Albinism. Of all the theories, albinism appears to be the most likely and most credible of the theories above. Since none of the others are observable phenomena and the albinism theory is observable and therefore provable.

That is to say, that while White European people proclaim their origins are in Greece, this cover story could be read as an avoidance tactic for not confronting the true meaning of skin whiteness which is as a result of mutation and a very real genetically deficient state from the black norm - or the 'hue-man' (man of colour) norm.'

Welsing goes on to define racism as experienced by the Hebrew in her book; the Isis Papers where she explains racism as such; *"Functional Definition Of Racism = White Supremacy = Apartheid: As a black behavioral scientist and practicing psychiatrist, my own functional definition of racism (white supremacy) is as follows:*

"Racism (white supremacy) is the local and global power system and dynamic, structure, maintained by persons who classify themselves as white, whether consciously or subconsciously determined; which consists of patterns of perception, logic, symbol formation, thought, speech, action, and emotional response, as conducted, simultaneously in all areas of people activity (economics, education, entertainment, labor, law, politics, religion, sex, and war).

For the ultimate purpose of white genetic survival and to prevent white genetic annihilation on planet Earth – a planet upon which the vast and overwhelming majority of people are classified as non-white (black, brown, red and yellow) by white-skinned people, and all of the non-white people are genetically dominant (in terms of skin coloration) compared to the genetic recessive white-skinned people."

It is therefore clear that deep within the unconscious psyche of the European collective mind there is an awareness; of their origin among Africans, and that with Africans as their fore-parents it means that whites were the offspring of Blacks that suffered from the skin condition of Albinism.

Does God love the white mice any more than the black mice or black people more than white people? The answer is of course no, "all mice are created equal". Nevertheless, some mice appear to be a mutation of the normal mice (a mutation is not necessarily an improvement). Being different has its benefits and its disincentives or costs also. In this case, it means genetic information has been lost.

It is noticeable that in white or lighter skins that there is a deficiency in melanin within the skin that results in an inability to handle strong sunlight. But the scientific teaching that white skin is the result of adaptation to the cold is a definite lie because there are myelinated people such as Eskimos who have been living in very cold regions for centuries and have neither turned white or been unable to deal with the cold; and if they are white-skinned today, it's due to miscegenation or cross breeding.

In an article by Rick Weiss, about work at Penn State University DNA research that was led by Dr Keith Cheng he *"Suggests that skin-whitening mutation occurred by chance in a single individual after the first human exodus from Africa, when all people were brown-skinned.*

That person's offspring apparently thrived as humans moved northward into what is now Europe, helping to give rise to the lightest of the world's races."

Weiss goes on to write, *"It's a major finding in a very sensitive area," said Stephen Oppenheimer, an expert in anthropological genetics at Oxford University, who was not involved in the work. "Almost all the differences used to differentiate populations from around the world really are skin deep."*

He further says, *"The work raises a raft of new questions -- not least of which is why white skin caught on so thoroughly in northern climes once it arose. Some scientists suggest that lighter skin offered a strong survival advantage for people who migrated out of Africa by boosting their levels of bone-strengthening vitamin D; others have posited that its novelty and showiness simply made it more attractive to those seeking mates."*

The article ends with a warning, *"Leaders of the study, at Penn State University, warned against interpreting the finding as a discovery of "the race gene." Race is a vaguely defined biological, social and political concept, they noted, and skin colour is only part of what race is -- and is not."*

The article can therefore be said to actually back up the mutation theory fully, meaning that whether it started in one person as an adaptation to survival or whether an entire group was modified to ensure their survival, Dr Cress Weling's work is well substantiated by the work at Penn State University and as such is being built on with important implications for the white Europeans populations everywhere.

Implications such as how they can deal with the calcification of their pineal gland which to a greater or lesser extent according to the lightness of the skin has ceased to function. Since the pineal gland is known to control creativity, dreaming and inventiveness, then there is an assumed reduction in creativity of those who have less melanin in their skin as opposed to those that have more.

Albinism is often thought of as something that happens among black Africans, but it's not that simplistic. This mutation actually happens among all nations and people groups whether light skinned or dark skinned. It occurs in nations with thin lips and straight noses such as the Asian Indians and Pakistani's of the Indian subcontinent as well as Africans and Europeans or lighter skinned people too (e.g. Irish or Nordic people).

We know that albinos tend to suffer with vision problems, including blindness, which is often associated with albinism, while Albinos do not necessarily all have vision problems, albinos must be very careful in the sun and wear sunglasses to protect their eyes, and sunscreen to protect their skin as many albinos and white people who don't classify themselves as albinos need to take the same protective measures because they share the same problem traits as Albinos with the same suffering of skin cancer due to the sun's ultra-violet rays affecting them both.

One very candid observation is that, "*Skin cancer resulting from exposure to the sun is the most common cancer in the world and it exclusively plagues white-skinned people.*" The website, 'LetspleaseGod.com' goes on to say, "*While albinos must protect themselves from the sun, Cancer.org doesn't mention albinism, but rather that white-skinned people in general are at risk (pale skin, natural red and blonde hair).*"

In 2003, Israel was rated the second highest in the world behind Australia for skin cancer. In their article it mentioned that exposure to the sun was the main cause of skin cancer. So my point is: white skin is an abnormality, it is albinism, it's a disorder, it's a weakness, and it's certainly not a trait of superiority.

Yet white people are never told this. Perhaps if the truth was taught, there wouldn't be so many cases of skin cancer. But telling the truth about white skin would destroy the concept of white superiority. For non-white people, if the truth was out, some would begin to learn to accept their skin colour, and thank God for their melanin.

While albinos are not what white people consider themselves to be (due to their programmed superiority complex), I believe they have this disorder by the cancer stats alone, but if some whites are not direct albinos, then many of them are very much descendants of such people.

What I mean by descendants is that they are the offspring of the breeding of albinos with dark-skinned nations to produce people with a tad more melanin in the body resulting in a very light tan color and darker hair and eyes as opposed to the standard pale skinned appearance you see in Irish people:

Basically white people (albinos) are becoming extinct and I believe I understand one of the reasons. As we know, melanin aids in human reproduction and albinos have very little of it, thus the decline in reproduction. It's just that simple to me.

Let's just face it, the perpetuation of this abnormality will not be allowed to be continued by nature. It's simply not natural to begin with. Just like there are very few albino animals in the animal kingdom, likewise the same is true among humankind. White people have always been a minority in the world since the beginning and now they're on the decline"

From the Bible's point of view, white skin was a bad thing, where it was either the result of leprosy or the end of the process of becoming a clean leper. A clean leper was someone who'd become completely white-skinned after the disease had run its course. At this stage, the disease was no longer contagious, but the person remained white. They were considered "clean", but not healed and would have to live in this state until death or a miracle occurred.

A clean leper would have looked like an albino and some could argue that this is the beginning of the so called "white race." But we know that there were clean lepers long before Gehazi was cursed and long since it has also occurred repeatedly. So while that may have been a factor it's not the only one. Nor is it a satisfactory answer to the overall problem of white skinned European origin.

The authors of the site, *"Real world history"* make a compelling case when they write that, *"Basically, Europeans come from East Indian albinos. Even today, East India continues to produce the most albinos of all lands and long ago these particular albinos decided to interbreed among their own kind.*

Eventually these people migrated to Europe which they later called home. Some bred with the Africans that had migrated there first, and this is where you get the not-so-pale-white European nations we see today." For real history and origins on the world's civilisations (and not just the false teachings coming from Europeans), I encourage you to visit www.realHistory.com.

Now a fraction of the human race is actually white or light skinned so it becomes an important question to ask, how or why is it that a group that is less than 15% of the population of the world controls so much of the resources of the world, while 85% or more of Earth's population is controlled by this dominant group?

If you examine the media, you will find that less than 15% of the population of Earth are on the media 85% of the time or more, while the converse is true of the people of colour as represented by the 85% only appear on the Media a small percentage of time.

This dominating by force is exactly as prophesied by the Bible, which is that Japheth would live in Shem's land and take it over as though he were Shem **Genesis 9:27**, *"God shall enlarge Japheth, and he shall dwell in the tents of Shem; and Canaan shall be his servant."* Since Japheth was considered a gentile and Shem a Jew, those who currently live in the land of Israel being they are Japhethites means that they are Gentiles even as prophesied by Yahoshuah.

In **Luke 21:24,** *"They will fall by the sword and will be taken as prisoners to all the nations. Jerusalem will be trampled on by the Gentiles until the times of the Gentiles are fulfilled."* The Jewish Japhethite insistence on dominating the land of Israel will one day come to an end, for even as the captivity was prophesied for the true Jew, so the return, restoration and the giving of justice has been prophesied also.

All bad things come to an end, **Ezekiel 4:13** prophesied our demise saying, *"The LORD said, "In this way the people of Israel will eat defiled food among the nations where I will drive them."* Thankfully for us, He has also promised to turn things around.

Jeremiah 23:7-8 *"So then, the days are coming," declares the Most High, "when people will no longer say, 'As surely as the Most High lives, who brought the Israelites up out of Egypt,' - but they will say, 'As surely as the Most High lives, who brought the descendants of Israel up out of the land of the north and out of all the countries where he had banished them.' Then they will live in their own land."*

We shall not only live in our own land, but the nations that have enslaved us shall become our servants and I can assure you that we shall be kinder to them than they have been to us. This is not based on my imagination or wishful thinking, but on solid Word based prophecy. If it were up to me, I would forget about the debt and let it go, but Yah has different ideas which He has broadcasted as prophecy.

We read in **Isaiah 14:1-3** the Word that Elohim promises, *"For the Lord will have mercy on Jacob, and will yet choose Israel, and set them in their own land: and the strangers shall be joined with them, and they shall cleave to the house of Jacob.*

And the people shall take them, and bring them to their place: and the house of Israel shall possess them in the land of the Lord for servants and handmaids: and they shall take them captives, whose captives they were; and they shall rule over their oppressors. And it shall come to pass in the day that the Lord shall give thee rest from thy sorrow, and from thy fear, and from the hard bondage wherein thou wast made to serve," Its coming and there is nothing that can be done to change this fact.

Quiz 7

1. What is the meaning of the word 'Human'?

2. What did Elohim create man out of?

3. Which of the theories of skin change is most credible?

4. What is the name of the scientist that put forward the mutation theory of skin change?

5. What is the name of the animal that was the flagship of albinism?

6. What is the most notable problem faced by albinos and their European counterparts?

7. Which country produces the most breeding albinos that look like Europeans?

8. Who did the Bible say would live in the territory of Shem?

---

1. Man of colour
2. Dust or soil
3. Albinism
4. Dr Frances Cress Welsing
5. Snowflake
6. Skin cancer
7. Pakistan
8. Japheth

Discussion

1. What is your perception of the balance of the amount of people in the world by skin colour, who is more and who is less?

2. How many races of people do you think are in the world today and why?

3. Did Elohim define men by race or nations and why do you think that is?

4. Who does the identification of men by race benefit and how?

5. How can we change the current racism in the world today as a group?

6. How can we apply this change to our life personally?

7. What is the biggest lesson of this discussion for you?

CHAPTER 8
WHAT ARE THEY AFRAID OF

It would appear that what is really behind the unreasonable fear that white people have about black people but especially black men is linked to having their irrational fear exposed for what it really is, overt and covert racism. The website, 'Dame Magazine' examined the portrayal of racism in the film: "Get out" which dealt with the many issues brought to the surface by racism what can happen is the subject matter of the film.

In the article about the film, the issues tackled reflect the 'mine-field' that the star of the film has to negotiate during the film. In it the writer says, "I know I could identity with what the film portrays, so here are the Chris encounters that I've personally experienced (Warning: SPOILERS!):

1. Finding out that your close friend or lover had not bothered to tell their family they were bringing a Black friend home and when asked to accommodate, told that to do so would be divisive or a racist act in itself? CHECK!

2. Being harassed by the police and watching a white ally come to your defense with a level of aggressiveness that would have gotten you shot? CHECK!

3. Showing up in a completely white establishment where the only other Black people around are servants? CHECK!

4. Making an effort to humanize those Black servants and forge relationships with them and face sideways

glances and strange quips from white counterparts while Black servants make an effort to further separate themselves from you in public for the sake of their own job? CHECKERONI!

5. Being told by a white person that they voted for Obama? OH HELL YES, CHECK!

6. Being physically felt up and thus objectified for your perceived athleticism? CHECK, HONEY!

7. Dealing with anti-blackness from Asians? CHECK!

8. Being repeatedly asked to speak for the Black community about our trials and tribulations despite the fact that it is quite clear there is only one acceptable answer and that answer is that racism is over and Black people are just trippin'? CHECK!

9. Being repeatedly gas lighted by your white "ally" and told that you're "looking for a reason to be mad"? Calling a Black friend in private to vent and listen them tell you to get your Black a** out of there?

10. Feeling obligated to soothe white ally's feelings when they realize you've been right all along? The ultimate betrayal of white ally when shit gets real? Being told it's not about race when it's clearly fucking about race? CHECK! CHECK! CHECK! CHECK! CHECK! CHECK!"

Most black people have encountered more than one of these issues during their time in white social circles at some time or another. Some have been unfortunate enough to experience most or all of these things. One thing is for sure, the experience is not pleasant, nor comfortable, but it is actually and entirely racist and should never have happened at all in the first place but it does.

Racism is the exercise of prejudice with power to enforce those prejudiced perceptions and that by definition means that only the dominant people group in any society can be racist. In most societies this means European or lighter skinned people today that have the dominant economic power to back up their prejudiced perceptions and are able to enforce their perceptions against the non-dominant others who happen usually to be black.

An example of this would be the problems encountered by black men where the fear of the dominant society is leading to the killing of black men as sanctioned by the system (I say this because not many if any police are being disciplined for the killings that have occurred to date).

In an article dealing with the fear of black men that are killed Philando Castile the writer says, *"The racist fear of Black men affects people of colour, even Blacks, as well as Whites. What makes the fear racist, it's not the skin colour of the people who have the fear, but the skin colour of the people who are taught to be afraid of black men.*

This, I believe, is why the jury acquitted Officer Yanez: They believed he was fearful. But his fear was not reasonable; it was (the fear that is) racist. That same fear has been killing and enslaving Black men for centuries and it is continuing to kill and enslave Black men today.

That fear of Black men is the same fear which killed Emmitt Till 60 years ago. It is the same fear which was fostered by slave owners in the antebellum period, by Jim Crow lawmakers after that, by opponents of Civil Rights in the 20th century. And it is the same fear which props up systemic racism today. And we need to confront this fear if we are ever going to overcome it.

Now, at this point, you may be thinking that statistics support the fear of Black men. You may be thinking that Blacks are statistically more likely to be violent or to commit murder. And then I point you to the statistics which show that the vast majority of homicide victims are killed by people of their own race, both Blacks and Whites. If you're White, you are many times more likely to be hurt or killed by a White man than a Black man. He further writes, Our fear of becoming victims are actually turning Black people into the real victims"

Going back to the previous writer from the film 'Get out', s/he wraps up the point about racism very well by saying that, *"The delegitimizing of our cultural differences will never be anything but infuriating. Living off our expense is every bit of insidious, abusive and slimy as Jordan Peele frames it to be. Racism is our devil babies and our ghouls. Racism is insidious, disarming, strange, infuriating, multi-generational, and unrelenting.*

Racism is more than enough to drive one insane, and it does. It leaves its victims of all colours dizzied. Its anti-blackness has forced Black folks into a hypnosis whereby our collective consciousness is shackled in deep space while neurosurgeons transfer the souls of nice white liberals into our bodies for white comfort." In other words, part of the fear is based on jealousy about the physique, intellectual brilliance and cultural richness brought to society by black people. The other part is just pure envy and bloody mindedness.

Tavis Smiley at a lecture at Lehigh University Pennsylvania said something which is worth quoting, *"While I'm not an angry black man, I do have a righteous indignation that burns inside me about the myriad of injustices that result in a daily contestation of people's humanity.*

The question is whether that feeling of being left out or left behind will be channeled into love and justice or hatred and revenge? I told the students at Lehigh that evening that I'm going with unarmed truth, unconditional love and being creatively maladjusted to injustice."

He was then asked a question that threw him totally and which I believe is quite pertinent at this time. *"Mr. Smiley, do you believe that given the crisis state of our democracy, we black folk could ever find ourselves enslaved again?"* Whoa! *Didn't see that one coming; did you?*

Neither did the mostly white audience. A quiet fell over the room. I swallowed hard. Looking directly at the student, I could see he was dead serious, and I wanted to treat his question with the soberness it deserved. But, truthfully, I stumbled as I began to respond, not knowing how to properly frame my response. My answer was? Yes."

There is a very real risk that so called, 'Democracy could be reversed because of its inherent unfairness and its inability to meet the needs of any host population while meeting the needs of the 1%.' I don't want to sound like a prophet of doom, but this can only mean a move towards dictatorial rule by the ruling class and a subjugation of those at the bottom of the social pile and that means persons of colour are about to experience even more oppression and potential enslavement.

The racist reactions of 'Europeans' is apparently endemic as demonstrated by a recent study, *"Published by the American Psychological Association, and based on the results culled from 950 online participants, the study found that both black and white people overestimated the physicality of black males when compared to white males of the same size.*

But it also found that only whites would be more likely to label them as more "dangerous" and to believe that authorities are more justified in using force to subdue them. (Additionally disturbing, is that the CNN writer must have assumed that all CNN readers are white, since she wrote that "we" find black males scarier)".

"Unarmed black men are disproportionately more likely to be shot and killed by police," says John Paul Wilson, PhD, of Montclair State University, a lead author of the study. He said, *'And often these killings are accompanied by explanations that cite the physical size of the person shot.'*

It's definitely not the first time researchers have proven the power of internal racial bias. Scientific findings have been around for decades, but first really captured public attention in 1998 with the release of the Implicit Association Test, which opened so many people's eyes to their own internal racial biases." The most relevant point of this article was, *"Both white and black subjects saw black men as bigger; only whites saw them as more threatening."*

The issue of racism leads us nicely into the racist mechanisms that have been devised to control the multiplication and rise of persons of colour to a place of equality through **Agenda 21.**

The Freedom advocate website outlines several objectives of agenda 21 which are as follows:

1. To reduce the population by 95 %
2. To implement a step-by-step approach to the abolition of privacy, private property, cash and private transportation.
3. To promote the relocation of people from rural areas to Smart Growth urban centres while monitoring and controlling their movements through technology.
4. To conscript public-private partners and mandate community volunteerism.

The above are the main goals but by no means the only goals as it would appear that the main people to be affected by this global, national, regional and local strategy to reduce the world population disproportionately will be the Hebrews and other people of colour.

Michael Shaw of Freedom advocate believes there is a new global policy on the block, *"Instead, a new philosophy with an accompanying action plan has been inserted; One that intends for humans to take on the status of livestock."* This sounds harsh at first, but the implications for persons of colour are horrendous since we are usually at the bottom of the social pile and this was the philosophy adopted during slavery, the likelihood therefore is that our people will once again suffer the most.

There are three broad principles that underpin Agenda 21:

a) First there is a step by step program for the abolition of private property.

b) Second is education (brain washing) for global citizenship. Do you think the notion of unalienable rights is present in today's schools? Take notice of the number of young Sustainables, many of whom identify themselves as Global Citizens.

c) The third driving principle of Agenda 21 is: Control over human action. For instance, we see technological advances being used by governments to monitor the individual in the pursuit of the exercise of their liberties.

They are using technology of all forms to accomplish this: Drones, biometric identification (preferably on or in your body,) cameras, GPS, internet health records, monitoring, police, private security, body grabbers and scanners, satellites, smart phone apps, Government databases, smart meters and smart money. Once these principles are operating fully, there will no longer be any freedom and for some there is no life because they will have been killed off also.

For the Hebrew, this time is called Jacob's troubles because it will affect us directly and be a time of direct assault on the Hebrews. This is also the time called by the Christians 'Mark of the Beast'. It is a destined time for the confrontation of the system that is being constructed by the Jewish Elites and will occur especially between the Kingdom of Yah and the Elites. What is required are prayer, fasting and evangelisation in order to slow this down so that people will have time to come to know the true and living Elohim.

Currently a staggering 85% of the world is represented by people of colour and only small factions are Europeans or lighter skinned people. What this means from the world of Eugenics (depopulation by any means necessary) is that out of a possible 7 billion people, some 6.5 billion of the people are likely to be persons of colour and likely to the subjects of an attempted cull.

You may never have considered it, but there is a Melanin genetic war on, where certain European elites do not want to be intermixed. The so called Jewish people are Europeans and have made it clear that while they are to remain 'racially pure' all other people are to intermix and homosexuality which limits procreation is to be encouraged. Think about it, if homosexuality becomes the norm whichever sex practices it, then there will be a fall in birth rates. This is at least true for most ethnicities, but is not the case among the 'Jewish people'.

In terms of the Melanin wars, if there was to be an intermixing of bloodlines amongst all peoples on the planet, the European would disappear because of their recessive genes and the world would look a lot darker. This means that European elites have something to protect and that is the survival of their race.

I believe that it is for this reason on the surface that persons of colour are the center piece of the assault called Agenda 21. However there is another reason and it is that the seed of the Serpent is fully against the true seed of Elohim and wants to kill them, indeed irradiate them from the earth if at all possible. This will never happen, because Yah has promised to return before it all comes to pass.

Elohim made a promise to Abraham in **Genesis 12:1-3** that He will bless him, and no matter how many people are against you, once Elohim decides to bless you, then no one can stop Him. The Bible says, *"Now the Lord had said unto Abram, Get thee out of thy country, and from thy kindred, and from thy father's house, unto a land that I will shew thee:*

And I will make of thee a great nation, and I will bless thee, and make thy name great; and thou shalt be a blessing: And I will bless them that bless thee, and curse him that curseth thee: and in thee shall all families of the earth be blessed."

This is a scripture to the true Hebrews and not for the Jewish people. And again in **Genesis 17:1-9** it goes on the give more specifics when it says, *"And when Abram was ninety years old and nine, the Lord appeared to Abram, and said unto him, I am the Almighty God; walk before me, and be thou perfect. And I will make my covenant between me and thee, and will multiply thee exceedingly.*

And Abram fell on his face: and God talked with him, saying, as for me, behold, my covenant is with thee, and thou shalt be a father of many nations. Neither shall thy name any more be called Abram, but thy name shall be Abraham; for a father of many nations have I made thee. And I will make thee exceeding fruitful, and I will make nations of thee, and kings shall come out of thee.

And I will establish my covenant between me and thee and thy seed after thee in their generations for an everlasting covenant, to be a God unto thee, and to thy seed after thee. And I will give unto thee, and to thy seed after thee, the land wherein thou art a stranger, all the land of Canaan, for an everlasting possession; and I will be their God. And God said unto Abraham, Thou shalt keep my covenant therefore, thou, and thy seed after thee in their generations."

Just knowing that Elohim made a promise must increase the feel good factor that exists in the midst of all this bad news about racism, eugenics and Agenda 21's execution. For though the news appears to be all bad, Elohim is on our side and so we cannot lose, no matter how bad it appears to get. You can depend on Him to deliver just what He says as He always has in times past for He is faithful and can never fail.

It is us who must be reprogrammed for success in the light of what we have seen and heard. We must understand that Elohim has equipped us with the information in advance so that we can be steadfast during our days of trial that are ahead.

We can also take some practical steps to address the problems that exist, but in the firm knowledge that we can only slow these things down and not stop them because Elohim has destined that these things should come to pass so that He may deal with them directly and supremely as the Elohim of all the Earth.

It is this truth that changes perception, because the perception of our suffering is that it will have a purpose and an end. The perception of our work is that this age or period of time is winding up and coming to an end.

The perception of our success is that we are not helpless but we can pray and take righteous action, committing ourselves to Elohim and knowing it will work out on our behalf in the long run. It is these happenings that comfort us and encourage us that the Bible is our book and is true so it cannot fail us. What it has promised will come to fruition.

We can therefore take a more personal stance with the Bible and apply it to our given situations knowing that prophetically and practically it must come to pass. The knowledge gained in the search of who Elohim is and finding out that He has chosen to identify with us is specific and certain knowledge and knowledge is power.

Power that empowers us to make changes that are needed in our personal lives and the communities in which we live so that we are able to love them like we should and thereby fulfil our mandate to be lights to the World.

Quiz 8

1. What is the bottom line of what white Europeans are afraid of about black people?

2. Define racism!

3. What is the main goal of Agenda 21?

4. What status does the ruling class assign to the human race?

5. What name does the Bible give to the time when Agenda 21 will be fully implemented?

6. What are three practical steps that the writer suggests are important in this timespan?

7. What is the Hebrew mandate?

---

7. Prepare
6. Pray, fast and evangelise
5. Jacob's troubles and Mark of the Beast
4. Livestock
3. Depopulation
2. Prejudice backed up by power
1. Fear of reprisal

Discussion

1. What do you notice about the fears nurtured by Europeans about black people?

2. List and define the kind of fears held by Europeans about black people.

3. Compare their fears with the reality and how many of them are actually based on facts?

4. Is there anything more that black people can do to make white people more comfortable around them?

5. Who really owns the problem and needs to do something to change the current situation and how?

6. How does Agenda 21 fit into all of this and what are its implications for black people?

7. What is the take home value of this discussion for you?

CHAPTER 9
THE DEVIL HAS A PLAN

A man was browsing the internet and saw a new type of gadget (phone). He felt that he just had to have it despite the fact that he only went on the internet to check his email. When he told his wife he had bought the phone, she said, "Why didn't you just say, get thee behind me Satan?" He said, "I did, however I clearly heard my voice say, that I really needed it."

That's how the devil operates, he will speak to you in your own voice and convince you that sinning is logical and in your own best interest. Sin is the first step in the devil's plan. His plan to steal, kill and destroy all Hebrews, because they represent the essential ingredient in Elohim's plan to save all of mankind.

Strategy 1 – Temptation through sin

From the time of the original sin by Adam and Eve till now, mankind has become subject to sin and slaves to Satan. His number one tool for causing Believers to fall and be kept enslaved is temptation to sin (**1 Corinthians 10:12**) for we are born in sin and shaped by iniquity.

All have sinned at some point and continue to practice sin unless they have made Messiah their Lord and Saviour. Satan knows that the wages of sin is death and excitedly tempts us so that we can get the wages of joining him in the lake of fire. For the purpose of temptation is to disqualify us from entering the Kingdom of Heaven because of sin (**Romans 6:23.**)

Indeed our sins will separate us from Elohim because He is too holy to behold or have sin in His presence for He is a holy Elohim. We must therefore not be ignorant of Satan's strategies (**2 Corinthians 2:11**).

Temptation operates like this:

- ✓ Satan baits the hook of temptation in order to approach you according to your weaknesses.
- ✓ Satan subtly undermines Elohim's Word.
- ✓ Satan will then accuse Elohim of something in your mind.
- ✓ Satan will always imply the consequence outlined by Elohim is too harsh.
- ✓ Satan will promise fun, but never mention the cost.

To overcome temptation

1. Remember temptation is not sin

2. Guard your weakness and strengthen the same

3. Have Elohim's Word in your heart and use it

4. Know and believe that Elohim always has your best interests at heart whether He appears to be acting with you or against you.

5. Understand Elohim is a God of His Word, He says what He will do and does what He says.

6. Understand that the cost of fun is always more than you can afford.

Strategy 2 - Murder or persecution

All murderers, persecutors and terrorisers are by definition usually planned, barbaric, well-funded, well-organized and deliberately formidable, as a foe both to democracy and our brothers and sisters in Christ around the world.

This strategy of killing whosoever would oppose their Satanic agenda for progressive evil is the next thing the devil uses out of his tool box if you prove to be a challenge to his authority. He will seek to arrange for someone to kill you or at the very least to make your life difficult.

This is what is happening currently in the USA, because the Hebrew brothers and sisters are seeking to affect positive change and many brothers are awakening, Satan has enlisted 'white supremacy' to work on his behalf and kill the black males. This has been given a special focus, so that their awakening can be stopped and efforts to keep the males alive will outstrip any activities that lead to awakening or spiritual consciousness.

The current top 5 on the world's watch list for persecution in order of severity are: North Korea, Somalia, Afghanistan, Pakistan, Sudan. The top countries on a watch list for genocide are:

First Syria who ranked sixth for persecution. Second is Sudan who ranked fifth for persecution. Third is Iraq, who ranked seventh for persecution. Fourth is Somalia that ranked second for persecution and fifth for genocide is the Central African Republic that currently ranks thirty fourth on the list of top fifty persecutors.

Do you begin to see a correlation between those who are being persecuted, murdered or targeted for genocide. You should, for wherever there is a move of Elohim or a spiritual awakening the enemy moves to stop it through persecution or murder.

Murder as a strategy is even more subtle, because you have countries in which religion is not restricted but the body count for murder is very high. For instance take: Number one is Honduras. Number two is Venezuela. Number three is Belize. Number four is El Salvador. Number five is Guatemala. All of whom are countries with religious freedom and a large contingent of Hebrew people.

You may not be surprised to know that all of these countries are developing nations in South America and that they represent some of the most religious nations on the planet.

However you may be surprised to know that most of the developed nations that are high in the table for murder? Are countries that are either in Africa, the Caribbean or South America, all places where the true Hebrews or persons of colour currently reside.

Nothing has changed, the great dragon is seeking to kill the children of the woman (**Revelations 12:1-12**) He will do his best to get others to Kill you physically or through some form of persecution that he has invented or stirred up. Persecution, hatred and murder by violence are very real strategies to stop believers from serving Elohim.

Strategy 3 - Is about getting people to give up on the faith because it's become all too much

When Satan attacked Job personally, it was about getting him to curse Elohim and die. So many because of trials and tribulations have come to the point where they get so stressed out that they gave up on believing Elohim has their best interests at heart and became despondent, fearful and even discouraged.

The most notable issues that arise from this strategy are pure tiredness of mind, body and spirit. When a person is tired of going from one battle to the next, one problem to the next and one challenge to the next, it is always a danger that they will be stressed out, burned out and give up.

Firstly never spread yourself too thin - always concentrate on working in your area of strength. Secondly be sure to spend time with Elohim in worship and prayer. Thirdly ensure that you take regular rest at least once per week (Sabbath). Next build a capable team to help you with the things that are not your core strength. Remember if someone else can do it, someone else should take care of it.

Next remind yourself that a tired or weary you is a dangerous you, so stay fresh with plenty of rest and recuperation time. Tired people make mistakes ask Job and ask David. Then do it differently by ensuring you get enough rest and that you are focused on the right task at the right time.

Finally, Deal with disappointments properly: The offenses and betrayal caused by done to others must be addressed quickly. Forgive them from the heart unconditionally. No one can afford to allow anger and frustration to linger and grow in their hearts or it will lead to their personal destruction.

Strategy 4 - Is to get you to kill yourself or turn on someone you love.

According to webmd.com, Suicide is the third leading cause of death for people ages 15 to 24 and the second leading cause for people ages 25 to 34. So it would appear that the purpose of the devil is to take out as many young people as possible as early as possible and you can be sure that many of these will be true Hebrew people.

The enemy wants you to kill yourself and waste your talent. He wants you to leave planet Earth before you accomplish your life purpose. This happens often around young lives who can see no hope for the future or older people who find themselves alone, with serious financial problems or even terminally sick.

The other group that tend to be targeted are those who suffer from depression and oppressive mood swings that over shadow them and lead to serious self-esteem complications that make their life appear unbearable to them and thus worth ending in their tiny minds that have not truly considered the eternal consequence of going to hell.

This strategy demands that the person under attack see themselves as worthless and of no value so that they are unable to see even the value of their own lives (priceless) and determine to end it. It is meant to blind them to the miracle working power of Elohim and the fact that they are just one divine intervention away from their personal deliverance.

Now it's logical that anyone who doesn't mind ending their life should think the same about the lives of others. So the strategy of suicide is linked to that of abuse, where often the abused become the abuser and the one that will kill self becomes the killer of others (think about Columbine).

It is observable that often among the so called 'mass murderers' that such persons will often kill others and then top it off by killing themselves. They first turn on someone they love or hate and then follow through after abusing or killing those around them who remind them of their abusers with the grand finale of taking their own lives in pointless suicide.

The thing to remember is that the enemy is behind all of this and is the only winner when someone kills or is killed by another. The purpose of Satan is to steal, kill or destroy lives and the more destructive he can be, the happier he is. Our stance against these strategies must be firstly awareness and secondly prayer and fasting.

We have spiritual power because we are the people of Yah and we must use this power against the strategies of the Enemy. Our Elohim overcame every one of these strategies in the person of Yahoshuah through obedience to the Word. Sometimes we come up against the strategies of the Enemy but are not filled with the Word and therefore yield to our feelings rather than fight through obedience to the Word.

The one thing the Enemy cannot overcome is a heart that is committed to obeying Elohim our God despite the personal cost to ourselves. We must be willing to go through it to get to it. Go through temptation to get to overcoming. Go through potential murder or persecution to get to glory. Go through stress to get to peace. Go through temptation to kill self or others to get to submission to Elohim. It is only by such submission that we will be able to complete our life's mission.

Quiz 9

1. What are the four strategies of the Devil to bring down humanity?

2. Of the strategies, which is the most effective and consistent one?

3. Which strategy is most prevalent in today's society against Hebrews?

4. When Satan baits a hook, what does he always bear in mind?

5. Which strategy employs stress as its key component?

6. If the devil can convince people to kill their own babies in the womb, what has he actually killed?

7. What kind of murder is suicide?

---

1. Temptation, murder or persecution, Stress, Abuse or suicide
2. Temptation
3. Murder
4. To suit your weakness
5. The problem to problem strategy
6. Stopped the potential and future of a nation
7. Self murder.

Discussion

1. Define murder.

2. What have you noticed about how the devil goes about causing people to fall into sin?

3. Compare temptation with suicide and which do you think is the worst sin to fall by and why?

4. If a person makes up their mind to live right, what kind of negative things tend to happen in their lives?

5. How should a person respond to the things that happen in their lives whether good or bad?

6. How can we apply these lessons to our lives?

7. What is the most important thing you feel you have learned from this discussion?

CHAPTER 10
WHAT THE BIBLE SAYS ABOUT GOD AND HIS PEOPLE

Let me make it clear from the onset that all people have originated from the same source (Adam) and all races are made in the image of Elohim (**Acts 17:26**). However in a study of Noah's descendants by, 'Christians on the net' the website says, *"The Bible does not explicitly give us the origin of the different "races" or skin colours of humanity.*

In the beginning, there was only one race because every human being was a descendant of both Adam and Noah. Admittedly, there could be much diversity in skin colour and other physical characteristics but still there was only one race.

Genetic research shows the possibilities of hybridization and breed development through selective pairing. Highly selective pairing among humans (such as marrying people with similar characteristics such as living habits or intelligence) might have facilitated the development of racial diversity.

For example, if those who were more physically active married other physically active people, the new families might become doubly more physically active than the rest of the people. Eventually, they would become a distinct group. As a result of this process, many distinct or diverse groups might form out of the original single race. These groups later became different races.

Another possibility is that Adam and Eve possessed the genes to produce children with different skin tones. This would be similar to how a mixed-race couple often has children that vary greatly in colour from one another."

Later, the only survivors of the Flood were Noah and his three sons and their wives, eight people in all (**Genesis 7:13**). Perhaps Noah's, Shem's, Ham's, or Japheth's wives were all of different races. Maybe all 8 of them were of mixed race, which would mean that they possessed the necessary genes to produce children of different races."

Of course the most likely scenario is that they had a mixed heritage with a predisposition towards certain colours as demonstrated by their descendants. Footnote 10 by TFE Publishing adds to the case by saying, *"Skin colour and other racial characteristics are a matter of certain genes being turned on or off while genetic information in the human gene pool is continually being lost.*

For example, brown eyes are the result of certain sections of the gene code being turned on to permit melanin to be produced in the skin and in the eyes to give the brown coloration. When that part of the code is turned off or lost, little or no melanin is produced and blue eyes and white skin are the result.

Therefore, when both parents have blue eyes that particular part of the code to produce melanin is absent and their child will have blue eyes. When one parent has brown eyes and the other blue, the dominant gene is brown and the children's eyes are more likely to be brown.

These rules are based upon the greater tendency for loss of genetic information rather than exchange i.e. it is not possible to acquire information once loss has occurred, which is the situation with two blue-eyed parents.

But information can be gained from a partner who already has that information i.e. the brown-eyed parent. All this being said, it might be supposed that Adam was the blackest of black but this does not 'necessarily' follow.

The most predominant colour among the world's people today is brown and from brown it is possible to get black. Adam and Noah and his family were almost certainly 'or likely' brown.

Undoubtedly, the concentration or loss of information occurred during the dispersion of the families, following the affair at the Tower of Babel. Social preferences would play a significant part in producing the various racial characteristics we see today and there is some evidence that adaptation to geographical location has an effect."

The Book of Enoch appears to suggest that the pre-flood world was a very melanised place. While the book of Enoch is not officially considered to be a part of the scriptural cannon, it holds an important enough place in the ancient world to have been part of the preserved books among the "Dead sea scrolls" in the cave at Qumran and must therefore be given serious consideration.

Concerning Noah's birth Enoch observes, "After a time, my son Methusalah took a wife for his son Lamech. She became pregnant by him, and brought forth a child, the flesh of which was as white as snow, and red as a rose; the hair of whose head was white like wool, and long; and whose eyes were beautiful. When he opened them, he illuminated all the house, like the sun; the whole house abounded with light.

And when he was taken from the hand of the midwife, opening also his mouth, he spoke to the Lord of righteousness. Then Lamech his father was afraid of him; and flying away came to his own father Methusalah, and said, I have begotten a son, unlike to other children.

He is not human; but, resembling the offspring of the angels of heaven, is of a different nature from ours, being altogether unlike to us." - **Book of Enoch 105:1-3**

The issues raised by this text are as follows:

1. Noah was born with white at least very fair skin.

2. Noah did not have the same appearance as other humans of his day.

3. They were aware of sexual relationships with angels

4. Lamech believed Noah was the son of an angel.

5. The fear was that Noah was not human.

6. The text further implies that children of angels and Nephilim were white

7. And that white skin was not common amongst the then current population it still isn't today where some 85% of the world are still persons of colour.

Lamech's recorded words were, *"being altogether unlike to us"* this can be seen as evidence that proves Noah was very different from those around him, especially his skin colour.

The description given to Noah in the Book of Enoch makes him the first documented so called albino or white man. However even though he was definitely a mutation on the then black or dark skinned majority he was still a member of the human race. Yes!

Although Noah is described as being white (like a European) we know that it is not just Europeans that have white skins or albinism. Black people can also be born with white skin and are then referred to as 'albinos'. However the truth is that white people are exactly the same, it's just that this truth has been downplayed.

My logic is therefore, "If Enoch, Lamech, and Noah were all from the line of Seth (Adam's third son). Then they were likely people of colour, it also stands that Seth was a man of colour, which would also make Adam a man of colour. Going forward this would make Ham, Shem and Japheth men of colour also. Since Shem was a man of colour, this makes the linage of Shem that of men of colour.

The above mentioned facts are reasonable conclusions based solely on the text presented and what is to follow. Which now brings us to a most controversial conclusion as to where this evidence points. For since Adam was created in the image and likeness of Elohim.

The image and likeness of Elohim is therefore that of dust (black or at very best brown skinned) and that makes God's image that of a black man. Now this is not written as a prejudiced statement, but as one of fact.

For I started this extrapolation by stating all men are made in the image of God (Elohim) and that we are all made from one blood. We are, but to be very specific, the black man was first and all others have come from him so the very specific image of Elohim is black. God is a black man!

The website, 'God on the net' has outlined correctly the origin of nations very succinctly from their fountain heads (Ham, Shem and Japheth) as follows, "According to **Genesis 9:19** and the Table of Nations in **Genesis 10**, all mankind is descended from the sons of Noah: Shem, Ham and Japheth.

For some strange reason, Noah's sons are always listed in that order although **Genesis 10:21** says Japheth was Shem's older brother. Normally in the Bible sons are listed in chronological order but the order must be indicative of Elohim's choice for the double portion blessing.

The descendants of Japheth settled in Anatolia, modern Turkey, and from there moved into the Caucasus mountains of Western Russia (this aptly describes the Ashkenazi) and from there settled Europe and Russia. They are the ancestors of the Caucasian peoples. Their main impact on Israel was through the Persians, the Greeks and the Romans.

Ham's descendants became the various black peoples who settled the African continent and parts of the Arabian Peninsula. His sons were Cush, whose descendants settled in Ethiopia, Mizraeim, whose descendants settled in Egypt, Put, whose descendants settled in Libya, and Canaan, whose descendants settled in Palestine and founded the cities of Sidon, Tyre and Carthage and, among others, were the ancestors of the Phoenicians."

The website goes on, *"Shem's descendants became the Semitic peoples who settled parts of the Arabian Peninsula, including what is now Saudi Arabia, Yemen, Jordan, Israel, and Lebanon. They were of a generally (thought to be) medium-brown complexion with facial features roughly mid-way between typical negro and typical Caucasian and the languages they spoke included Arabic, Hebrew, and Aramaic, Jesus' (Yahoshuah's) native language."*

I would like to agree with the first of the two comments and disagree with the conclusion about the Shemites (Semitic) peoples. I have a number of reasons for disagreeing with the conclusion that Semitics are simply people of a medium brown complexion.

While Shem's descendants were and are the Semitic peoples, the Semitic people were originally black (which incorporates the darkest black and the lightest of brown complexions) and the whiter skins in the area today are only due to conquest by the Greeks, Romans and other European imports into the region.

For its worth noticing that:

1. There are no European or light skinned persons who are naturally occurring in Africa (Israel is in North East Africa).

2. The region from which the Semites arise is: Assyria, aka Asshur, aka Mesopotamia, aka Babylon, aka Sumaria, aka Ur of the Chaldees or Chaldea (all the same country). If you look up the ancient people of that area/ country, you will find that they were black people.

3. "Zondervan's Compact Bible Dictionary: Ham – The youngest son of Noah, born probably about 96 years before the Flood; and one of eight persons to live through the Flood. He became the progenitor of the dark races; not the Negroes, but the Egyptians, Ethiopians, Libyans and Canaanites." What that credible source just admitted was that there were two black races (The Hamitic (Indigenous African blacks and the Negros).

4. Since Shem is the father of the Negros and Negros are black people then Shem was black. Since Eber and Abraham (and Sarah too) are descended from Shem and come from the same region above, then they too were black. So we can safely say that the line of Shem is black contrary to popular scholarship and opinion which appears to be somewhat warped and bias in favour or the European opinion.

5. Abraham as you have already found out was from Ur, a city of Chaldea. The Chaldeans were known to have been a black people; they are in fact the ancestors of the people of Chad today. They still exist and they are as black as it gets.

Let us take on board the issue of the current 'Jewish' people (so called). According to the website *'Ebos are the real Hebrews'* the writer expresses himself and I agree to the fact that, *"Jewish people are descendants of Ashkenaz who is Japheth's grandson from his first son Gomer (**Genesis 10**). The Bible says the sons of Noah bear names according to their families and the Jewish people still are called by their father's name Ashkenaz today.*

Modern Jewish scholars claim that Ashkenaz is the Hebrew name for Germany and refers to Jewish people who lived in Germany or the Rhine-lands but that they are from Israel as opposed to Sephardic Jews who they claim are from Spain. That's not correct – for some simple reasons:

First, when Gomer named his son Ashkenaz, there was no Germany. Second, why would Hebrews in the bible – who were proud of their heritage as children of Shem – allow their name to be associated with someone like Ashkenaz who is not their ancestor, but a descendant of Japheth?

Also, most Jews are Ashkenazi Jews and they are all from around the Caucasus area not only the Rhineland. There are Ashkenazi Jews who are from areas far from the Rhineland like Russia, Romania, Bulgaria, Yugoslavia, Poland etc. and this includes the so-called Sephardic Jews.

From this, one can see that "white" people today in general are children of Japheth which makes sense because they inherited the colder lands. Simple biology will tell you that cold climate facilitates the comfort of white skin while tropical climate makes human skin black or tanned due to melanin activity and UV exposure."

The writer of that article hit the nail on the head squarely by clarifying for us that there is no genetic, ethnic or genealogical reason why the white European Jewish person would be a part of the Semitic heritage of the descendants of Shem. None whatsoever!

Quiz 10

1. How many races are made in the image of Elohim?

2. What causes colour and skin tone?

3. What is the dominant colour of the people of the world today?

4. From whom do all men descend?

5. Who does the book of Enoch make the first white or albino man?

6. Where on the planet are white and lighter skins predominantly from?

7. Where on the planet do darker skins naturally occur?

8. From whom do the Hebrews descended?

9. From whom are the Ashkenazi descended?

Discussion

1. What are your observations about skin colour?

2. What do you think is the least numerous of the three groups of people (Shemetic, Hametic and Japhetic) and why?

3. Compare white and black people and what are the similarities and differences?

4. Define Ashkenazi? Define Jew and explain how if at all the two terms, 'Ashkenazi Jew' do or don't belong together?

5. What is the practical application of what you have discovered in this discussion?

6. What will you remember most from this discussion?

CHAPER 11
THE GREAT PRETENDERS AND THE BIBLICAL REALITY

There is however a prophetic reason why they now pretend to be Jews according to scripture. The first is a prophesy about the actual occurrences of the end times. Read the following from, **Genesis 9:27**, *"God shall enlarge Japheth, and he shall dwell in the tents of Shem; and Canaan shall be his servant."* Elohim knew that Japheth would take over Shem's land or territory and this has come to pass in our days.

Luke 21:24 makes it clear that the people in control of Jerusalem in the end times will be gentiles. *"And they shall fall by the edge of the sword, and shall be led away captive into all nations: and Jerusalem shall be trodden down of the Gentiles, until the times of the Gentiles be fulfilled."*

The second reason is prophetic acknowledgement by Yah that He is aware of the deception of the Japhetic Jewish people of the end time. Read these two scriptures and honestly examine your conclusions.

Revelation 2:9, *"I know thy works, and tribulation, and poverty, (but thou art rich) and I know the blasphemy of them which say they are Jews, and are not, but are the synagogue of Satan."* Elohim apparently has a problem with them that 'say they are Jews but are not'. These people are said to worship in a very specific worship place a 'Synagogue'.

It's not just a one off, because Elohim reiterates on the matter in **Revelation 3:9**, "Behold, I will make them of the synagogue of Satan, which say they are Jews, and are not, but do lie; behold, I will make them to come and worship before thy feet, and to know that I have loved thee." The people who are living the lie are those who worship in a synagogue.

The people who will be worshipped according to that scripture above will be Elohim's true people the true Hebrews. From this, we can definitely conclude that the current Jews are neither Hebrew nor true Jews. They are Japhetic and pathetic because they are pretenders and deceivers according to the Word of Elohim.

Based on this and other information, it is impossible for Shemites to have been white or for Abraham to have been white and the father of the "Jewish" people of today which leads us into the genealogy of the descendants of Abraham who must also follow the pattern and be black or brown skinned since the linage of Abraham, Isaac and Jacob continue to be Shem(itic) = Semitic.

According to the website, 'apologetics index.org,' "*It has been confirmed that the ancient Sumerians were akin to the modern Black Dravidians of India. The Sumerians also had an affinity with a people known as the Elamites, the very first Semitic group mentioned in the Bible (**Genesis 10:22**).*

The Elamites were a black-skinned and woolly-haired people as the colorful glazed artwork on the royal palace walls of the ancient Persian city of Susa clearly show. Thus Abraham, the native of Sumerian and the founding father of the Israelite nation, was a black man. The black racial origins of the Patriarchs is not based on mere conjecture, it is in complete agreement with the picture one gets from examining the identity of the earliest inhabitants of southern Mesopotamia."

Judah had five children and they were all males, (**1 Chronicles 2:4**), three were by his first wife and two were by what was initially his sons wife (**1 Chronicles 2: 3-4.**) Both of his wives were descendants of Canaan, who was a black man that was the son of Ham (see **Genesis 10:6**).

Tamar, Judah's second wife, bore him two of these sons whose names were Phares and Zarah so returning to the genealogy, Judah married one Hamitic (indigenous African) but had children with both black women and is himself black (Semitic) so his descendants will be black.

Rahab is a Hamite also and therefore black but a fore parent of King David of the tribe of Judah (**Joshua 2:1 and 6:25-27**). She came from Jericho a city of the Canaanites. She was therefore a Hamite or African woman, but she is a fore parent of King David in Judah's linage.

Ruth in the linage of Judah is a Moabitess so is a descendant of Lot (Semitic) so she is black like Abraham. Given that she is of the same origin as the true Jews and likely mixed with Hametic Africans, she is undoubtedly black. She too is in the linage of King David as his grandparent. So this makes King David of whom it is said that he was, 'ruddy' or red skinned, a red skinned black man.

Solomon who is born of Bathsheba and David is described in scripture to have been a black man and can be verified to have been the fore father of the great King Haile Selassie who was a black Emperor (see **Songs of Solomon 1:5.**)
Mary and Joseph are both of the tribe of Judah and therefore for the reasons already explained (Judah and the wives with which he had his children were black) were also both black because the line of Judah were all black.

Christ too is of the linage of Judah, born of a black mother and has a black step father (Joseph) so Messiah is also black (God is a black man). Now Messiah's family goes to hide from Herod and were instructed by Yah to go hide in Egypt – **Matthew 2:13** (Kemit – land of the burnt faces). Only burnt faces can hide in the land of the burnt faces and not be spotted. So they also had to be black.

Of the Hebrew people in time of famine it said, "Their visage is blacker than a coal; they are not known in the streets: their skin cleaveth to their bones; it is withered, it is become like a stick." **Lamentations 4:8**.

What do we find in the book of Isaiah about the colour of Messiah? It uses the same term for his time of suffering. **Isaiah 52:14**, "*As many were astonied at thee; his visage was so marred more than any man, and his form more than the sons of men:*" Instinctively, I believe this passage is referring to the same phenomena. When Yahoshuah took on the sins of the entire world, He became blackened by sin and His appearance was like no other man's had ever been.

What we find in the book of Daniel sitting on the throne of Elohim is a black man called the ancient of days. **Daniel 7:9-10**, "*I beheld till the thrones were cast down, and the Ancient of days did sit, whose garment was white as snow, and the hair of his head like the pure wool: his throne was like the fiery flame, and his wheels as burning fire. A fiery stream issued and came forth from before him: thousand thousands ministered unto him, and ten thousand times ten thousand stood before him: the judgment was set, and the books were opened.*"

In a second scripture in the Book of Daniel we pick up on the scene as **Daniel 10:5-6**, *"Then I lifted up mine eyes, and looked, and behold a certain man clothed in linen, whose loins were girded with fine gold of Uphaz: His body also was like the beryl, and his face as the appearance of lightning, and his eyes as lamps of fire, and his arms and his feet like in colour to polished brass, and the voice of his words like the voice of a multitude."*

Let us now move swiftly to the scripture that contains both scenes in one place.

1. You will see the ancient of days and learn His identity

2. You will see the white garment, the woolly hair, the burnt (beryl or burnt brass body)

3. You will see the burning eyes and the voice like a multitude all of which proves it's the same person.

Revelation 1:12-18, *"And I turned to see the voice that spake with me. And being turned, I saw seven golden candlesticks; And in the midst of the seven candlesticks one like unto the Son of man, clothed with a garment down to the foot, and girt about the paps with a golden girdle.*

His head and his hairs were white like wool, as white as snow; and his eyes were as a flame of fire; And his feet like unto fine brass, as if they burned in a furnace; and his voice as the sound of many waters And he had in his right hand seven stars: and out of his mouth went a sharp twoedged sword: and his countenance was as the sun shineth in his strength.

And when I saw him, I fell at his feet as dead. And he laid his right hand upon me, saying unto me, Fear not; I am the first and the last: I am he that liveth, and was dead; and, behold, I am alive for evermore, Amen; and have the keys of hell and of death."

The identity of the one who is in this vision is already revealed in the **8th verse** of the same chapter. *"I am Alpha and Omega, the beginning and the ending, saith the Lord, which is, and which was, and which is to come, the Almighty."*

This is how we know it is the Ancient of Days, but we also know it is Yahoshuah making the claim to be Almighty Elohim. This is further confirmed by **Revelation 4:8**, *"And the four beasts had each of them six wings about him; and they were full of eyes within: and they rest not day and night, saying, Holy, holy, holy, Lord God Almighty, which was, and is, and is to come."*

Now, the Greek historian Herodotus visited Egypt in the 5th century B.C. He came into contact with EGYPTIANS and described them as DARK-SKINNED and WHOLLY HAIRED. Herodotus wrote: *"For the people of Colchis are evidently Egyptian, and this I perceived for myself before I heard it from others.*

So when I had come to consider the matter I asked them both; and the Colchians had remembrance of the Egyptians more than the Egyptians of the Colchians; but the Egyptians said they believed that the Colchians were a portion of the army of Sesostric.

That this was so I conjectured myself not only because they are DARK-SKINNED and have CURLY HAIR (this of itself amounts to nothing, for there are other races which are so), but also still more because the Colchians, Egyptians, and Ethiopians alone of all races have practiced circumcision from the first."

So in conclusion of this chapter, it is clear from a wealth of sources that the Semitic people were always and will always be black. Biblically it is also conclusive that the Ancient of Days (aka God) is a black man and that Yahoshuah who is the visible representation of the invisible Elohim was and is a black man too because there is but one God (Elohim) and He sovereignly chose to come into this world as a black man for His own sovereign reasons.

Someone said, "The greatest form of flattery is imitation, to which I say, 'It's good to be one of the originals'." There is no doubt in my mind that the original Semites are the black of the Caribbean, the Americas and those found in other parts of the world where Yah has taken them.

There is also no doubt in my mind that Yah and his human manifestation are also black even though some try to change His colour and His people. Another person said that, "The grass is always greener on the other side of the fence," well I have come to share that it's our grass and that's why it looks so much greener that other people are willing to lie, steal or pretend that it's their grass and contrive evidence to prove the same.

Quiz 11

1. The word 'Semitic' is equal to what word?

2. Who are the people who will be worshipped in Revelations 3:9?

3. According the where the Hebrews came from, is it possible for them to be the white Jewish people of today?

4. The Elamites are described as what kind of people?

5. What was the origin of Judah's wife?

6. Rahab, Ruth and Solomon are all of the linage of Judah according to the Bible? What Colour were they by definition?

7. What colour was Yahoshuah aka Jesus?

Discussion

1. What do you notice when you look at the country from which the Hebrews originate?

2. When you look at Judah and his wives, what colour children must they have had and why?

3. Compare the Children of Judah and the Children of Ashkenaz and what will be the major differences?

4. How can you prove that Messiah had to be black?

5. How is this information important to other black people today?

6. What is the thing that most impresses you about today's discussion?

7. How will you implement what you have learned in your life?

CHAPTER 12
UP IN HEAVEN

In **Isaiah 6:1-3** we find, *"In the year that king Uzziah died I saw also the Lord sitting upon a throne, high and lifted up, and his train filled the temple. Above it stood the seraphims: each one had six wings; with twain he covered his face, and with twain he covered his feet, and with twain he did fly. And one cried unto another, and said, Holy, holy, holy, is the Lord of hosts: the whole earth is full of his glory."*

In the day when your prejudices and everything that hinders you from worship dies, you will see Yah as He truly is, 'High and lifted up'. For in heaven, the worshipers recognise Him as the only one who is truly holy and therefore worthy of worship. In fact the very essence of worship is bowing down before the Creator. Worship involves two things: The first is that we must bow ourselves down as creatures, and the second is that we must lift Him up.

That is what worship is all about. It is the exalting Elohim and the humbling of ourselves. The English word for worship comes from an old English word worth-ship. It attributes worth to Elohim.

It exalts Elohim as the Most High and that is exactly how we should see Elohim worshipped in the Scriptures. Blessed be Elohim. The angels ascribe blessedness, holiness, majesty, and praise to Him, might, power, wisdom, honour, and glory belong to Elohim because His the God.

His attributes and His characteristics are worth consideration and as it is we are humble to mere creatures in His presence. The creature is put in his place of lowliness and the Creator is dignified. As we stop and contemplate, and meditate on the majesty of Almighty Elohim, we are embarrassed in His presence. It exalts the Lord. When Isaiah saw the Lord high and lifted up it glorified God and made the man conscious of his humanity.

In Daniel and Revelations there is a worship scene set like that of Isaiah. In Revelation 4 the scene is in heaven -the center of which is the throne of Elohim. Let's read it, **Revelations 4:2-8**: *"And immediately I was in the spirit: and, behold, a throne was set in heaven, and one sat on the throne. And he that sat was to look upon like a jasper and a sardine stone: and there was a rainbow round about the throne, in sight like unto an emerald. And round about the throne were four and twenty seats: and upon the seats I saw four and twenty elders sitting, clothed in white raiment; and they had on their heads crowns of gold.*

And out of the throne proceeded lightnings and thunderings and voices: and there were seven lamps of fire burning before the throne, which are the seven Spirits of God. And before the throne there was a sea of glass like unto crystal: and in the midst of the throne, and round about the throne, were four beasts full of eyes before and behind.

And the first beast was like a lion, and the second beast like a calf, and the third beast had a face as a man, and the fourth beast was like a flying eagle. And the four beasts had each of them six wings about him; and they were full of eyes within: and they rest not day and night, saying, Holy, holy, holy, Lord God Almighty, which was, and is, and is to come."

Daniel 7:9, *"I beheld till the thrones were cast down, and the Ancient of days did sit, whose garment was white as snow, and the hair of his head like the pure wool: his throne was like the fiery flame, and his wheels as burning fire."*

Daniel 10:5-6, *"Then I lifted up mine eyes, and looked, and behold a certain man clothed in linen, whose loins were girded with fine gold of Uphaz: His body also was like the beryl, and his face as the appearance of lightning, and his eyes as lamps of fire, and his arms and his feet like in colour to polished brass, and the voice of his words like the voice of a multitude."*

Revelations 1:14-18, *"His head and his hairs were white like wool, as white as snow; and his eyes were as a flame of fire; And his feet like unto fine brass, as if they burned in a furnace; and his voice as the sound of many waters. And he had in his right hand seven stars: and out of his mouth went a sharp twoedged sword: and his countenance was as the sun shineth in his strength.*

And when I saw him, I fell at his feet as dead. And he laid his right hand upon me, saying unto me, Fear not; I am the first and the last: I am he that liveth, and was dead; and, behold, I am alive for evermore, Amen; and have the keys of hell and of death."

All heaven is in session and worships the one with the white woolly hair. The promise is that every knee will bow to God, but God turns out to be Yahoshuah.

It begins in **Isaiah 45:23**, *"I have sworn by myself, the word is gone out of my mouth in righteousness, and shall not return, That unto me every knee shall bow, every tongue shall swear."*

In **Romans 14:10-11**, we pick up the same scene, *"But why dost thou judge thy brother? or why dost thou set at nought thy brother? for we shall all stand before the judgment seat of Christ. For it is written, As I live, saith the Lord, every knee shall bow to me, and every tongue shall confess to God."*

In the next scripture we find out that it is Yahoshuah that every knew will bow to and that this pleases Elohim. **Philippians 2:9-11**, *"Wherefore God also hath highly exalted him, and given him a name which is above every name: That at the name of Jesus every knee should bow, of things in heaven, and things in earth, and things under the earth; And that every tongue should confess that Jesus Christ is Lord, to the glory of God the Father."*

Revelation 4:1-11, *"After this I looked, and, behold, a door was opened in heaven: and the first voice which I heard was as it were of a trumpet talking with me; which said, Come up hither, and I will shew thee things which must be hereafter.*

And immediately I was in the spirit: and, behold, a throne was set in heaven, and one sat on the throne. And he that sat was to look upon like a jasper and a sardine stone: and there was a rainbow round about the throne, in sight like unto an emerald.

And round about the throne were four and twenty seats: and upon the seats I saw four and twenty elders sitting, clothed in white raiment; and they had on their heads crowns of gold. And out of the throne proceeded lightnings and thunderings and voices: and there were seven lamps of fire burning before the throne, which are the seven Spirits of God.

And before the throne there was a sea of glass like unto crystal: and in the midst of the throne, and round about the throne, were four beasts full of eyes before and behind. And the first beast was like a lion, and the second beast like a calf, and the third beast had a face as a man, and the fourth beast was like a flying eagle.

And the four beasts had each of them six wings about him; and they were full of eyes within: and they rest not day and night, saying, Holy, holy, holy, Lord God Almighty, which was, and is, and is to come.

And when those beasts give glory and honour and thanks to him that sat on the throne, who liveth for ever and ever, The four and twenty elders fall down before him that sat on the throne, and worship him that liveth for ever and ever, and cast their crowns before the throne, saying, Thou art worthy, O Lord, to receive glory and honour and power: for thou hast created all things, and for thy pleasure they are and were created."

In Revelation 11 the scene is heaven again. The twenty-four elders, who represent the church of God, do what they always do in Revelation-they always fall on their faces and worship God.

In **Revelation 11:17-18** they worshipped Him and what did they say? *"Saying, We give thee thanks, O Lord God Almighty, which art, and wast, and art to come; because thou hast taken to thee thy great power, and hast reigned. And the nations were angry, and thy wrath is come, and the time of the dead, that they should be judged, and that thou shouldest give reward unto thy servants the prophets, and to the saints, and them that fear thy name, small and great; and shouldest destroy them which destroy the earth."*

Yahoshuah turns out to be a black man because the one who is being worshipped has woolly hair and only black people have hair described as being like wool. In that same passage, the one on the throne has feet burnt like fine brass and only black people have skin that appears to be burnt as dark as burnt brass. The image of the person is girth about the waist and having flashing eyes.

This is the same for both the vision of Daniel and the vision of John in Revelation:

- The apostles turn out to be black men
- The true Hebrew turns out to be a black man too
- There is a promise that one day everyone will hold on to the true Jew and want to follow them to the house of Yah
- There is a promise that the false Jewish people will worship at the feet of the true Jews.
- There is a promise that the enslaver will become a slave themselves

Someone said, that the Europeans should pray that we will be kinder as masters than they are to us. Elohim took the side of the under-dog in this struggle of nations and one day the under-dog will be in charge of all things.

Those who have mistreated and abused Elohim's people need to pray that we will be better masters when they become the servants of the Hebrew people (**Joel 3:6-8 and Isaiah 14:1-3**).

However in the final analysis sitting on the throne of God (Elohim) we find Yahoshuah and see Him for what He is: A black man.

Quiz 12

1. The first scene of worship is taken from which book of the Bible?

2. The third is taken from Revelation, from which book does the second scene or worship come?

3. What colour is Elohim when He is seen in the Old Testament?

4. What is the definition for the word, 'Worship'

5. What is the identity of Elohim when we find out who the person on the throne is in Revelations?

6. So what colour is God overall whether as the Father or in a flesh body?

7. For what does the writer suggest that Europeans pray in the light of the information revealed?

---

1. Isaiah
2. Daniel
3. Black
4. Worship
5. Yahoshuah
6. Black
7. That we are kinder than Europeans are to us

Discussion

1. What are your observations about the Colour of Elohim?

2. What would be your interpretation of Praise and how does that differ from Worship?

3. Compare the scene in Daniel 7:9 with that of Revelations 1:8,14-18 and what do you now see?

4. What is important to you about worship?

5. How can or should we worship Elohim?

6. How will you treat worship differently from the way you did before?

7. What is the one thing you will be taking away from this discussion above everything else?

CHAPTER 13
THE WHITE BOY'S TESTIMONY REVISITED

Young Billy whose apocalyptic vision we started this book with, had a seeming nightmare (to him) that God is a black man and it's true because history affirms this fact, the honest archaeology of the time confirms it to be true through paintings, statues and artefacts of ancient Semitic peoples.

The child's prophetic vision is similar to that which many other children are experiencing around the world and these agree with the Bible which upholds and confirms all of this information surgically.

Though Bible genealogy honest scholars can tell that God is a black man and that His people Israel have always and will always be black; despite the great deception currently being undertaken by the Ashkenazi (**Revelation 2:9**) this thing is not a secret.

Not hidden because current religious groups/ organisation, denominations and important individuals know the truth. The powers that be are trying to hide it, but God's definitely a black man and the cover up is failing to cover anything but rather revealing dishonesty and trickery are at play.

God has always been black because Adam the image of Elohim was a black or at best a mixed race man and you know that blackness is not judged by how white you are but by whether you have any black blood in you at all or not.

Every mixed race person knows that they are still considered black by their European counterparts and accepted as black by their black equivalents. So Adam was by definition a black man (for more about dominant genes see my book – Black skin royal identity).

God's people have always been a black people of Semitic origin, but you can't tell just by looking at their skin tone alone that they are Semitic only that they are black. The Semitic origin can therefore only really be determined by a look at their blood (DNA).

It's kind of like in the Old Testament where you could not tell who was a Jew just from the outside because you had to take a look at their private parts to see if they were circumcised to determine their affiliation.

Today it's even more private, because you can have two black people in front of you, but being black on its own doesn't necessarily make you a true Hebrew. It's clear to us that a Hamite and a Semite are two different kinds of people though both are black in skin colour and Hebrew distinction would require a closer examination (probably by DNA testing) to determine Hebrew origin.

The curses of Deuteronomy 28 and Leviticus 26 do conclusively single out the Semitic man and targets him for special treatment because he needs to return to the covenant and restore his relationship with Yah our Elohim.

It targets him and his descendants for either extermination or renewal because they alone of all the nations did He choose to know in that way (**Amos 3:2**).

Due to Father Abraham's relationship with Yah, Elohim has chosen to take on a people (having created a covenant with mutual obligations) and to come through their bloodline as a human in order to fulfil His promise to Abraham, Isaac and Jacob. It was Elohim Himself that bore our curse and carried our sicknesses (**Isaiah 53:3-7**).

This was done so that we would not have to bear those burdens and yet we still do what we do not need to do and suffer when we do not need to suffer and remain in an intoxicating forced sleep whereby we have been enslaved, abused and are still a suppressed and downtrodden people to this day.

Now I must make it clear that He didn't just die for the black man, but for all mankind (**John 3:16-18**). Messiah is not only the Elohim of the black man, but the creator of all men. He is concerned about the welfare of all men, but has placed a premium on His people Israel for the sake of His friend Abraham. He has chosen to suffer with His people and identify with their pain because He is compassionate and just.

Those who have treated His people badly will one day pay for it because of the universal law of sowing and reaping (**Galatians 6:7-9**). So the reparations that the enslaved have sought for centuries will never come by human struggle, but will come by divine judgement.

For those who recognise that they and their fore parents have sinned against Elohim and His people (the true Hebrews) there must be repentance, forgiveness and restoration.

For those who refuse to acknowledge their wrong, there can only be the servitude promised in **Isaiah 14:1-3,** *"For the Lord will have mercy on Jacob, and will yet choose Israel, and set them in their own land: and the strangers shall be joined with them, and they shall cleave to the house of Jacob.*

And the people shall take them, and bring them to their place: and the house of Israel shall possess them in the land of the Lord for servants and handmaids: and they shall take them captives, whose captives they were; and they shall rule over their oppressors. And it shall come to pass in the day that the Lord shall give thee rest from thy sorrow, and from thy fear, and from the hard bondage wherein thou wast made to serve"

Unless there is repentance there cannot be forgiveness. So many Europeans have benefited from the subjugation of the Semitic and Hametic peoples either directly or indirectly. Their exploitation of the countries largely made up of persons of colour has become a joke. We (the people of colour) have become the laughing stock of the 1% because of the ease of corruptibility due to money.

For they buy our leaders and our raw materials at less than cost through the corruption of our politicians and sell them the processed resources back at highly inflated prices or even gain ownership of the source assets themselves at the expense of the 99%.

The continued subjugation of a person because of either their skin colour or their genetics cannot go on forever. The plan of the Satan to eliminate a whole people group and other poor people through Agenda 21 cannot happen without consequences from Elohim who has taken note and will one day take action against those who abuse the poor of mankind both white and black.

One day not too soon from now, money will mean nothing, silver and gold will hold no value and greed will get its repayment, **James 5:1-8**, *"Go to now, ye rich men, weep and howl for your miseries that shall come upon you. Your riches are corrupted, and your garments are motheaten.*

Your gold and silver is cankered; and the rust of them shall be a witness against you, and shall eat your flesh as it were fire. Ye have heaped treasure together for the last days. Behold, the hire of the labourers who have reaped down your fields, which is of you kept back by fraud, crieth: and the cries of them which have reaped are entered into the ears of the Lord of sabaoth.

Ye have lived in pleasure on the earth, and been wanton; ye have nourished your hearts, as in a day of slaughter. Ye have condemned and killed the just; and he doth not resist you. Be patient therefore, brethren, unto the coming of the Lord. Behold, the husbandman waiteth for the precious fruit of the earth, and hath long patience for it, until he receive the early and latter rain. Be ye also patient; stablish your hearts: for the coming of the Lord draweth nigh"

God's a black man and one day real soon, He's coming back as Judge. To take vengeance on the abusers of the poor in order to set matters right in the earth (vengeance is mine He says – **Romans 12:19**). He asks us to be patient (waiting without agitation - sometimes for a long time). This means that when we look around, we will think it's time that He acted.

We will believe it's time that we did something or time that something was done on our behalf, even by any means necessary. This is not the way of Elohim. He instructs us to wait, because His judgement will be supernatural and final.

We must not run ahead of our Yah Elohim, but must be patient knowing that He who started this work will surely complete it. He is on your side, He is aware of your struggles. He identifies with your fight because God's a black man. So let me finish with this. The boy whose testimony opened this book was indeed a racist child, one who was being groomed by his parents to continue a tradition. However it's clear from his story that he will never be the same again.

Once you have come in contact with the true Elohim, you can never deny or say what others want you to say. Since Elohim has awakened me and opened my eyes, I cannot deny Him nor say He is not who He has clearly shown me that He is. God is a black man, and I will shout it from the highest building or peak. God is a black man and it matters because one day soon He is coming back.

So now you ask the so what question right? So what if God is a black man? The answer is that the reason He became black is that it's considered the lowest of the low. Since He is also the highest of the high, He covers all spectrums of mankind and that means that He is qualified to save everyone. (**John 3:16-18**).

As a result, all that would be saved must respond to Elohim's love by asking what they need to do and then obey the reply. The reply is found in **Acts 2:38** and involves three things. 1) **Repentance** (Turn away from sin and turn to Elohim). 2) **Baptism in the name of Yahoshuah** by full immersion in water. 3) **Infilling of the Holy Spirit** speaking in other tongues as they did on the day of Pentecost. This is for all nations, Jews and Gentiles. Then we must all serve Him and Him alone

Quiz 13

1. What kind of vision did young Billy and his dad think that he had?

2. What kind of archeology confirms the truth of what he saw?

3. What kind of scholars will say that God is black?

4. What do the curses of Deuteronomy 28 and Leviticus 26 do?

5. For which nation did Yahoshuah die?

6. What needs to be done if the cycle of becoming a slave is to be avoided?

7. What will happen to the rich who have cheated the poor and not set matters right?

---

1. A nightmare
2. Honest archeology
3. Honest ones
4. Pinpoint the true Hebrews
5. All nations
6. The offenders must repent and be reconciled to Elohim
7. They will be judged by Elohim

Discussion

1. How do you think what happened to Billy might have changed him?

2. Compare what he was like before the experience to how he is likely to have been after experiencing his heavenly vision?

3. How is Billy likely to see black people in the future?

4. How is Billy's experience likely to affect his family and friends?

5. What will you do differently as a result of what Billy experienced?

6. How will you apply what you have learned to your life personally?

REFERENCES

Books

1. The Holy Bible – King James Authorised verision

2. Ivanov, Vladimir. "Russian Icons" Rizzoli; New York, 1st edition 1990

3. *Sommers, Cecil. "Temporary Crusaders" John Lane publishers, London, 1919*

4. Morgan, James. "In the Footsteps of Napoleon" The Macmillan company, New York, 1915, p 85

5. Herodotus, "Complete works of Herodotus" delphi Classics, United Kingdom, 2015.

6. Cress Welsing, Frances. "The Isis Papers: The keys to the colours" Third World Press, U.S.A. 1991

7. National Geographic: Mar. 67, Oct. 70).

8. Agenda 21: The Earth Summit Strategy to Save Our Planet (Earthpress, 1993) and The Local Agenda 21 Planning Guide, published by ICLEI, 1996

Websites

1. Hadro, Matt. "Fox anchor defends white santa remarks" [website] http://www.newsbusters.org/blogs/nb/matt-hadro/2013/12/17/cnn-guest-says-depiction-white-jesus-has-been-used-kill-millions (accessed 8 July 2017)

2. Uygur, Cenk. "Jesus & Santa Are White - Megyn Kelly On Fox News" The Young Turks [website] https://www.youtube.com/watch?v=DBn2wIQWoB8 (accessed 8 July 2017)

3. Zinn, Howard. "History is a weapon" [website] http://www.historyisaweapon.com/defcon1/zinnslaem10.html (accessed 8 July 2017)

4. The editors Wikipedia, "Cotton plantation record and account book", [website] https://en.wikipedia.org/wiki/Cotton_Plantation_Record_and_Account_Book (accessed 8 July 2017)

5. Smith, Susan. K. "Whites and the Fear Caused by White Supremacy" Huff post [Blog] http://www.huffingtonpost.com/rev-dr-susan-k-smith/whites-and-the-fear-cause_b_8885126.html (accessed 8 July 2017)

6. Jensen, Robert. "What White People Fear" Yes magazine, [web article] Spring 2010, http://www.yesmagazine.org/issues/america-the-remix/what-white-people-fear (accessed 8 July 2017)

7. Holmberg, Tom. "Did Napoleon's troops shoot the nose off the Sphinx?" [website] http://www.napoleon-series.org/faq/c_sphinx.html http://www.napoleon-series.org/faq/c_sphinx.html (accessed 8 July 2017)

8. Editors of Stuppid, "Racist Boy Dies For 3 Minutes, Says Jesus is a N**ger." [website] August 19 2014 http://stuppid.com/racist-boy-dies-black-jesus/ (accessed 8 July 2017)

9. Editors of Artable, "Sistine Madonna" [website] 2017, http://www.artble.com/artists/raphael/paintings/sistine_madonna (accessed 9 July 2017)

10. The editors africanamerican.org, "The black Madonna in Europe" [website] http://www.africanamerica.org/topic/the-black-madonna-in-europe (accessed 9 July 2017)

11. Editors Christian Mystery Schools, Cults, Heresies, "Black Madonna" [website] http://www.unexplainedstuff.com/Religious-Phenomena/Christian-Mystery-Schools-Cults-Heresies-Black-madonna.html (accessed 9 July 2017)

12. Editors Cover gallery, "Black Madonna" Russian life Magazine, Spring 1995 issue [website] https://russianlife.com/chtenia/covergallerychtenia/ (accessed 9 July 2017)

13. Editors of Wikipedia, "Black Madonna" [website] https://en.wikipedia.org/wiki/Black_Madonna (accessed 9 July 2017)

14. Editors Catholic silent crusade, "Do Catholics worship images and statues" [website] http://catholicsilentcrusade.blogspot.com/2013/09/6 -why-do-catholics-worship-images-and.html (accessed 9 July 2017)

15. Rozett, Ella. "Black Madonnas and other Mysteries of Mary" [website] http://interfaithmary.net/pages/blackmadonna.html (accessed 9 July 2017)

16. Editors Missouri University, "Eastern orthodox icons" [website] https://maa.missouri.edu/sites/default/files/docents /easternorthodoxicons.pdf (accessed 9th July 2017)

17. Faith in YHVH, "Cesar Borgia" [website] https://faithinyhvh.wordpress.com/2011/01/29/cesar e-borgia/ (accessed 19 July 2017)

18. Detroit Baptist Theological Seminary, "Three differences between Eastern Orthodoxy and Roman Catholicism" [website] http://www.dbts.edu/2015/04/20/three-differences- between-eastern-orthodoxy-and-roman-catholicism/ (accessed 19 July 2017)

19. Isrealite.net, "Is this the image of Jesus" [website] http://www.israelite.net/image.htm (accessed 19 July 2017)

20. American bible society, "Blacks in biblical antiquity" [website] http://bibleresources.americanbible.org/resource/bla cks-in-biblical-antiquity (accessed 9 July 2017)

21. Weiss, Rick. "Scientists Find A DNA Change That Accounts For White Skin", Washington post [online article] December 16, 2005, http://www.washingtonpost.com/wp-dyn/content/article/2005/12/15/AR2005121501728.html (accessed 17 July 2017)

22. Editors of Kwing, "Study: Noah's descendants" [website] http://kwing.christiansonnet.org/courses/bible-gen/gen-21_ee.htm (accessed 17 July 2017)

23. Creation moments, "Noah's three sons" (Footnote 10), TFE Publishing, Ontario [website] http://www.creationmoments.com/content/noahs-three-sons (accessed 17 July 2017)

24. Black history in the Bible, "The Book of Enoch: Black Adam, Albino Noah, and The Image of God" [website] http://www.blackhistoryinthebible.com/hidden-history/the-book-of-enoch-black-adam-albino-noah-and-the-color-of-god/ (accessed 17 July 2017)

25. Editors of God on the net, "Jesus' Black Ancestors" [website] http://www.godonthe.net/wasblack.htm (accessed 17 July 2017)

26. Ebos are the real Hebrews, "Why Biblical Hebrews could not have been White People" [website article] http://www.ibosaretherealhebrews.com/why-biblical-hebrews-could-not-have-been-white-people/ (accessed 17 July 2017)

27. Editors 'Got questions.org', "Why did God choose Israel to be His chosen people?" [website] https://www.gotquestions.org/why-God-choose-Israel.html (accessed 17 July 2017)

28. Open doors, "World watch list", [website] https://www.opendoorsusa.org/christian-persecution/world-watch-list/?gclid=CjwKCAjw47bLBRBkEiwABh-PkTMfqrSfb4WUyHlYdsR3I0wCUBnCHA93cHGxaxfBFET4 kUtvWvyxABoCtiAQAvD_BwE#download?keyword=world %20watch%20list&b&g&171589115954&1t1&c&1741042 75&34353543033 (accessed 18 July 2017)

29. Genocide watch, "Countries at risk" [website] http://genocidewatch.net/alerts-2/new-alerts/ (accessed 18 July 2017)

30. Webmd, "Suicidal thought or threats overview" [website] http://www.webmd.com/mental-health/tc/suicidal-thoughts-or-threats-topic-overview#1 (accessed 18 July 2017)

31. Adams, Isaac. 9 Marks, "Why white churches are hard for black people" [website] https://www.9marks.org/article/why-white-churches-are-hard-for-black-people/ (accessed 19 July 2017)

32. Editors apologetics index, "Black Hebrew Israelites" [website] http://www.apologeticsindex.org/5864-black-hebrew-israelites (accessed 20 July 2017)

33. Halstead John, "Our Fear Of Black Men Is Racist, And It Killed Philando Castile" Published 22 Jun 2017, [website] http://www.huffingtonpost.com/entry/our-fear-of-black-men-is-racist-and-it-killed-philando_us_594aeb77e4b092ed90588b75 (accessed 21 July 2017)

34. Hood, Carol, H. "This Is Why 'Get Out' Is Freaking Out White People" Published 28 Feb 2017, [website] https://www.damemagazine.com/2017/02/28/why-get-out-freaking-out-white-people (accessed 21 July 2017)

35. Smiley, Tavis, "Why I Fear America Could Enslave Black People Again" Published 20 Oct 2016, [website] http://time.com/4535292/donald-trump-black-slaves/ (accessed 21 July 2017)

36. Steyels, Mike, "Study proves white people terrified of black people—again" Mass appeal, published 13 March 2017 [website] https://massappeal.com/study-black-males-size-overestimated-whites-view-threatening/

37. Shaw, Michael. "Regionalism the blue print for your serfdom" Published 28 September 2013 [website] http://www.freedomadvocates.org/regionalism-blueprint-serfdom/ (accessed 21 July 2017)

38. Shaw, Michael. "The ultimate war part 1" Published September 2012 [website] https://www.freedomadvocates.org/wp-content/uploads/2015/04/The-Ultimate-War-by-Michael-Shaw-Part-1_September-2012.pdf (accessed 21 July 2017)

39. Finley, Taryn. "Jesus wasn't white and here's why that matters?" Huffpost, published 22 Dec 2015, [website] http://www.huffingtonpost.com/entry/jesus-wasnt-white-and-heres-why-that-matters_us_567968c9e4b014efe0d6bea5 (accessed 27 Jul 2017)

40. Editors: Gotquestions.org, "Is Christianity a white man's religion?" [website] https://www.gotquestions.org/Christianity-white-religion.html (accessed 27 Jul 2017)

41. Editor: Lets please God, "Why I believe black people are the Israelites" and "Racism: The origin of white skin" [website] http://www.letspleasegod.com/2015/09/black-people-israelites-bible/ http://www.letspleasegod.com/2016/05/white-skin-origin-racism-pt11/ (accessed 27 July 2017)

Printed in the USA
CPSIA information can be obtained
at www.ICGtesting.com
LVHW021619141023
761108LV00010B/884

9 781548 644666